$\mathcal{C}$ontents

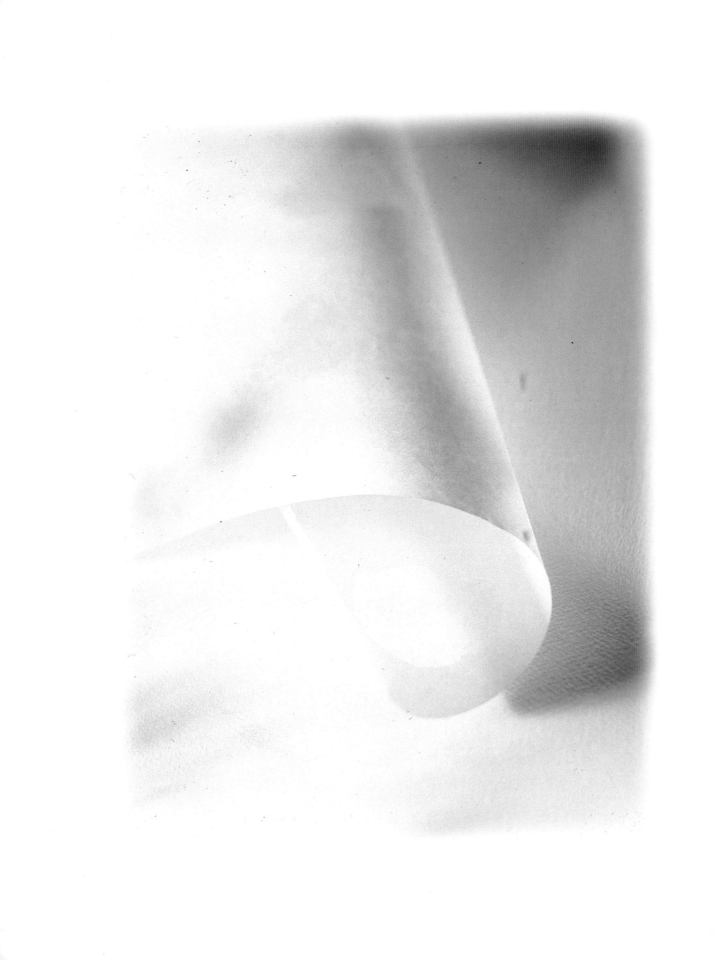

Making & *Decorating* Your Own Paper

Kathy Blake & Bill Milne

Innovative
Techniques
& Original
Projects

STERLING PUBLISHING CO., INC. NEW YORK

This is for all the people I love. You know who you are.
Kathy

For all the people who said, "You're *still* working on that book?"
Bill

Library of Congress Cataloging-in-Publication Data

Blake, Kathy.
      Making & decorating your own paper : innovative techniques & original
projects / Kathy Blake & Bill Milne.
               p.   cm.
          Includes index.
          ISBN 0-8069-0544-1
          1. Paper, Handmade.   2. Waste paper–Recycling.   3. Paper work.
I. Milne, Bill.   II. Title.
TS1109.B58   1994   93-45440
676'.22–dc20   CIP

10 9 8 7 6 5 4 3 2 1

First paperback edition published in 1995 by
Sterling Publishing Company, Inc.
387 Park Avenue South, New York, N.Y. 10016
© 1994 by Kathy Blake and Bill Milne
Distributed in Canada by Sterling Publishing
% Canadian Manda Group, One Atlantic Avenue, Suite 105
Toronto, Ontario, Canada M6K 3E7
Distributed in Great Britain and Europe by Cassell PLC
Wellington House, 125 Strand, London WC2R 0BB, England
Distributed in Australia by Capricorn Link (Australia) Pty Ltd.
P.O. Box 6651, Baulkham Hills, Business Centre, NSW 2153, Australia
Printed and bound in Hong Kong
All rights reserved

Sterling ISBN 0-8069-0544-1 Trade
          0-8069-0545-X Paper

All projects, execpt where noted, were made by Kathy Blake
All photos, noted or not, are by me. Bill

Making the Most of Paper

1

Paper, a relatively recent invention, has made possible the spread of information, ideas and art.

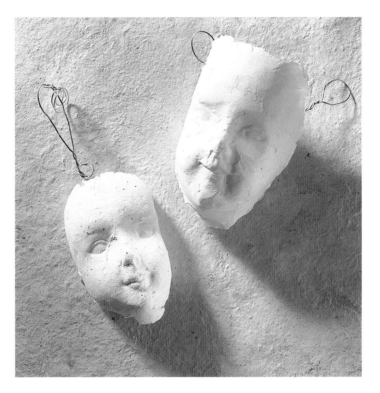

Paper—one of the most common of all commodities—passes through our hands in countless forms, as newspapers, brochures, computer printouts, photographs, restaurant menus, cardboard boxes, envelopes, books, and letters, to name a few. The relatively simple invention of papermaking has made the worldwide spread of information and knowledge possible for the past 2000 years.

We often take an abundance of paper for granted, but a few insights into the history and process of papermaking can increase our appreciation for this extremely useful and versatile material.

Stone and clay tablets, metals and fabrics were used for writing and drawing surfaces until people began making vellum from calf skins and parchment from sheep skins.

Then, at least 4500 years ago, Egyptians created papyrus, the precursor of paper—and the word from which "paper" is derived—from the inner layers of reeds. Strong and flexible, papyrus was used for record keeping and communication.

By 105 A.D. in China, T'sai Lun had developed a method of making true paper. He beat fishing nets and rope into a pulp, which he poured over a screen made of tightly tied bamboo strips. The water drained through the small holes between the bamboo strips, leaving a thin sheet of paper, which he left to dry. When it was dry, he peeled the finished paper off the

Today paper is still made from many of the same materials used by those who originated papermaking.

bamboo. As knowledge of the method spread through China, silk, plant fibers and wood pulp were used to make papers of various styles.

Japanese and Korean papermaking also began during the first century and, in that part of the world, became a fine art. The Japanese made papers that were so fine and strong they could be used for making lightweight, semi-transparent walls in homes. The finest papers were used for recording sacred texts and the lesser grades were used for money and wrapping.

It was a long time before papermaking knowledge traveled outside Asia's closed societies. The spread of this knowledge was helped along when, in 755 A.D., Arabs invaded Samarkand and captured Chinese papermakers who finally divulged their know-how. Once the Arabs learned the methods, papermaking spread throughout the Mediterranean region, east to India and west to Europe.

The need for paper remained limited until the invention of the printing press in the mid-15th century. Before that time, books were written and bound by hand and their circulation was limited.

Once entire pages could be printed on a press and books became less expensive to produce, paper was needed in large quantities and the paper industry was born.

Modern Papermaking

The earliest paper mills—from the 10th century through the 15th century—were very messy, unhealthy places to work. Huge vats of cotton and linen rags were left in water for weeks to rot and break down. Workers chopped the rags into tiny pieces. This slurry was then sent to a mill where it was mechanically mashed to break the pieces down to a consistency that could be used to form long rolls of paper using labor-intensive machines.

New papermaking inventions and innovations slowly made the process more mechanized and less messy. Even today, though, you know by the odor when you're within a few miles of an industrial paper mill. Machines produce paper by the same basic methods as paper is made by hand, but in incredible quantities and speeds. From pulp to mesh to felt to pressing and drying, all is done on Fourdrinier machines that can run at speeds of 3500 feet per minute, producing continuous rolls of paper 30 feet wide.

By the mid-19th century, wood pulp was more commonly used for papermaking. Cotton and linen are still used in top-quality papers—the higher the rag content, the better the paper quality and the lower the acid content.

Judging Paper Quality and Choosing Papers

There are three classifications of paper: machine-made, mold-made and handmade. Machine-made paper, by far the most common, includes newsprint and any other paper purchased on rolls, most drawing papers, cover stock, paper for printing mass-market books, photography developing papers and other papers used in huge quantity. Machine-made papers made with wood pulp content are high in acid, which causes the paper to become brittle and yellow.

Mold-made paper is also made by machine, but in smaller quantity. The machine moves more slowly, which affects the paper's fiber alignment. A cylinder revolves in a vat of pulp, the pulp attaches to a wire mesh on a cylinder, and then the cylinder is transferred to a moving felt for pressing and drying.

Handmade paper is made in the same labor-intensive method as it has been for centuries. Some art supply stores and specialty shops carry handmade papers and they are, understandably, expensive.

One sure way of finding the grainline is to tear a strip at the corner of the paper. If it tears easily, you have found the grainline. If the tear is jagged and difficult to keep straight, you've found the crossgrain. (If you've ever torn an article from a newspaper, you have experienced the feel of the grainline and crossgrain.) If you don't want to tear your paper, you can hold light- and medium-weight paper to strong light and look at the direction of the fibers.

Paper manufacturers indicate grain in the second dimension given on the paper's packaging. For example, paper labeled 14 × 17 inches (35 cm × 43 cm) has a grainline that follows the 17-inch (43 cm) side.

There are many, many choices available to us in the size, weight and quality of papers. Poster board, bristol, cover stock, watercolor, drawing, pastel, corrugated, newsprint, construction, tissue, gift wrap, typing, and kraft are some of the papers to use in art and craft projects.

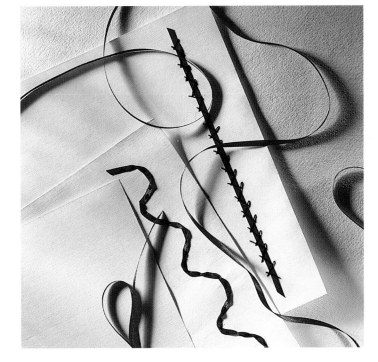

When choosing paper, remember that the best paper is the one that is appropriate for the project. Purchase or make the finest papers for items that you want to last for decades. Low-quality newsprint, construction paper and tissue papers are fine for short-lived uses.

With some patience and effort—but very little expense—you can make paper in a time-honored method for use in your own projects. See chapter 2, "Handmade Paper," on page 19.

Price is a reliable indicator of paper quality, but you can also judge quality by texture and appearance. The best papers are marked in one corner with the maker's logo, either a stamp or a watermark. Depending on the surface texture desired, the paper may be hot pressed between hot metal rollers for a smooth, slick texture, or to retain a rougher, more open surface, cold pressed or not pressed at all. Other finishes for good papers include embossing, laminating, coating, waxing and impregnating.

Finding the grain of paper is sometimes important, because paper tears, folds and bends much more easily when worked parallel with the grain. Also, the paper is stronger along the grainline. The grain of the paper is determined by the way the fibers lie, which is the result of fast-moving machines that pull and align them. Handmade papers, of course, don't have a distinguishable grainline, because the fibers crisscross.

Design Transfer Techniques

Regardless of what you were told as a child, you don't have to be able to draw to be artistic. Your own sense of color, line, form and design will make your projects unique and beautiful.

As you make paper projects, you will often find that the design takes on its own life and the results are much different from what you had planned. Enjoy the process and see what happens. The surprises are often very pleasant.

Sometimes, however, you may see designs that you want to reproduce as faithfully as possible. In these cases, there are several transfer techniques that can be used.

Tracing

Transferring a design from a two-dimensional object, such as a post card, poster, tablecloth, magazine picture, children's coloring book, or photograph, can be done effectively with tracing paper.

Use true tracing paper, as sold from art supply shops, or use any paper that is light enough to see through.

Place a sheet of tracing paper over the object you are copying, then with a heavy, dark line, draw around all the lines you need to capture the essence of the design. You now have the design on the tracing paper.

Tape the tracing paper onto a sheet of cardboard or onto a light source, such as a window or a light box. (You can make a light box of sorts by moving two chairs or tables of equal height close together, but with some space between them, then placing a sheet of clear or white acrylic over the space between. Tape your pattern on the sheet of acrylic, then place a lamp under it.)

Now tape the paper you will be decorating over the tracing paper. You should be able to see the heavy tracing lines through paper, so you can now draw those lines onto the paper to be decorated.

Copy machines

Take advantage of technology by copying designs on a copier. Many modern copiers will enlarge or shrink the size of designs. If you have a relatively small design and would like it bigger than the machine will enlarge, make a copy as large as possible, then place that copy in the machine and enlarge it again until it is as large as you like. Experimenting with shrinking and enlarging can result in interesting and inspiring effects.

You can also play with the dark and light options on a copier and change the appearance of a design dramatically.

The ink from a fresh copy can be rubbed onto another sheet of paper as a design transfer option.

Color copiers give the artist even more exciting options for copying designs to paper—collages, paper masks, greeting cards, book covers, and lids for boxes are some of the ways color copies can be used.

Adhesives for Paper

Your choice of glues and adhesives is important to the success and life of your projects. Again, the choice of glue depends on the project and the type of paper you use. Although there are exceptions, in general avoid rubber cement, library paste, glue sticks and clear, brown glues, because these adhesives hold only temporarily.

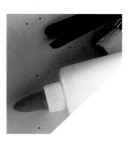

White glue is a good choice for most papers because it can be thinned with water when wet, and it dries clear and water resistant. Glue thinned with water to the consistency of thin cream is useful as a sealer on wood or to prevent polyurethane from discoloring paper.

Polyvinyl acetate (PVA) is a plastic-based glue that stays flexible when dry. Its color, consistency and characteristics when wet are very much like other white glues, but it is preferable for some paper projects, like flexible book covers and envelope seals. PVA can also be thinned with water and used as a sealer. It is sold under brand names and is available from well-stocked art supply stores and book arts suppliers.

When working with white glue or PVA for large projects, such as painting it onto sheets of paper, pour the glue out of its bottle into a shallow container or jar that has a wide enough mouth to allow a brush to be dipped into it. If the glue is too thick for the use you have in mind, mix it with water until it is the proper consistency.

For smaller gluing jobs, you must use white glue properly to prevent it from wrinkling light- and medium-weight papers. First, open the glue bottle with a pin so the opening is only the size of the pin to prevent a lot of glue coming out when you squeeze the bottle.

When gluing paper products, remember that the surface that receives the glue will expand when it gets damp with the glue, then contract as it dries. The thinner the paper, the more it will stretch and contract. In fact, even very thin paper glued and then applied to heavy cardboard can cause the cardboard to warp. So applying glue to the cardboard, rather than the paper, will help prevent warpage.

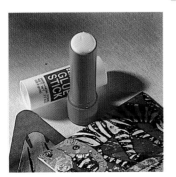

When gluing edges of paper together (for example, when making paper cylinders or gluing paper shapes onto a paper mask) very lightly dot the edge of the paper to be glued with white glue. With the edge of a piece of lightweight cardboard, squeegee the glue along the paper's edge. Lightly blot the glue with a piece of waste paper before sticking the edges together. This procedure will prevent glue from seeping out from under them.

To cover a cardboard box with paper, make light dots of glue over the surface of the cardboard, stipple the glue with an old paintbrush with stiff bristles right to the edge of the cardboard, then apply the paper to the surface.

Another way to adhere paper to cardboard is to make a mixture of half paste and half white glue. Apply the paste/glue mixture to the paper with a stiff-bristled brush in a very thin layer, then apply the paper to the cardboard. This method works well because the texture of the paste/glue mixture is drier than white glue, so the paper doesn't get as damp since it takes longer to dry than white glue, so you have more time to make adjustments.

Recipes for making paste

Flour Paste

This recipe makes about 6 cups ($1\frac{1}{2}$ L) of paste and it keeps in the refrigerator for up to 2 weeks. You can easily make half or a quarter of the amount if you like.

1 cup flour

1 cup cold water

4 to 5 cups boiling water

4 drops oil of cloves

Put the flour in a large saucepan and mix in the cold water with a wooden spoon to make a smooth paste. Place the pan over medium heat and gradually stir in 4 cups (1 l) of the boiling water. Stirring constantly, cook for 5 minutes. Gradually add more boiling water if the paste seems too thick. It will thicken slightly as it cools. Stir in the oil of cloves, which is an important preservative.

Starch Paste

This recipe makes only about $\frac{1}{3}$ cup (75 ml) of paste. It is a bit clearer than flour paste and can be used in the same ways.

2 teaspoons cornstarch

1 teaspoon flour

1/2 teaspoon powdered alum

1/3 cup water

In a small saucepan, mix together the dry ingredients. Stir in the water and cook, stirring constantly, over medium heat for 5 minutes, or until thick.

Handmade Paper

2

Most of the equipment needed for papermaking is readily available. Clockwise from top left: vat for holding pulp; household blender for beating pulp; "felts," which can be cotton, linen or wool fabric or nonwoven interfacing material; paper and cotton linter for making pulp; deckle and mold for forming sheets; a bag of paper pulp; sponge; plastic sheets to protect pressing boards from water; plywood boards and clamps for pressing wet sheets of paper.

Handmade Paper

The pleasures of making paper are manifold. Beginning with paper and fibers that would have been thrown away otherwise, you end with sheets of beautifully textured and colored paper. Soft-edged and speckled with shreds of threads, vegetable fibers, leaves or flowers, handmade papers give pleasure to the eye and hand.

While the satisfaction is great, the cost is low. Equipment needed for papermaking is inexpensive and most of the material is cost-free.

Throughout this book, you will find many ways of using the paper you make to create books, greeting cards and note paper, and to cover boxes, frames and picture mats. You can make original, artistic, crafted objects to use in your home or office, or to give as awe-inspiring gifts.

You also have the great satisfaction of making use of some of the piles of paper that accumulate in your home and office. Begin a collection of quality papers—including those with type and writing on them—such as typing, computer and copier paper and

business stationery that would go into the trash can, to be used for making your handmade paper.

Sometimes you'll find stationery thrown aside because it is slightly damaged or because an address or telephone number changes, making it obsolete. Hoard for future use any quality papers that come your way.

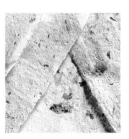

Quality In– Quality Out

The quality of the paper that goes into your handmade paper determines its strength and the length of its life. For best results, use paper with a high rag or cotton content with a "dry" texture. Staples, gums and glassine must be removed from all your paper before you use it.

Magazines

The pages of most magazines and color brochures have a glossy finish that gets gummy during the papermaking process. And, no matter how gorgeous the colors are on a magazine page, when they've been soaked and pulped, they inevitably turn gray.

If there are certain colors or small areas of design in magazine pages that you particularly like and want to use to decorate your handmade paper, snip them into tiny pieces and add them to the pulp just before forming the paper.

Newspaper

Newspaper, brown bags and telephone books, while abundant, aren't good choices for papermaking, because they have a high acid content which will destroy the handmade paper rather quickly.

Papers marked "recycled" usually contain newspaper and do not make satisfactory handmade paper, except for short-lived or practice sheets.

A deckle and mold are easily made from wood framing and wire screen or nylon netting.

Heavy papers

Cardstock, envelopes, heavy watercolor paper and bristol board can be used in papermaking, but should be soaked and pulped separately from other, lighter weight papers. Be sure to cut away all gummed edges and glassine windows from envelopes before soaking them. Because of their extra thickness, it takes more time and pulverizing to break down the fibers in heavier papers. Even with extra pulverizing, such papers may show up as thick spots in the finished paper. This can give it a nice texture, if that's the effect you want.

Type on paper

Type and writing on paper will often show in the finished handmade paper as tiny black or colored specks. Sometimes, if the paper has not been thoroughly pulverized, you can see whole letters in the finished paper.

Cotton linter

Cotton linter is made of 100% cotton fibers and adds strength to any paper. If you're making paper with material that has a high cotton content, you don't need to strengthen it with linter. But if you're using gift wrap, typing or computer paper, you have the option of adding about 25% or more cotton linter for strength.

Cotton linter is available from well-stocked craft and art stores in sheets or shreds. To use linter, tear sheets into stamp-size pieces

or tear shreds into small pieces, then soak them for at least 10 minutes before pulverizing them with other papers you have soaked.

For very strong, fine quality paper, you can use only cotton linter instead of pulping other papers with it. Cotton linter makes pure white paper that also takes dyes and additions very well.

Colored paper

Colored tissue paper, crepe paper and paper napkins are useful coloring agents for hand-made paper, because their dyes will bleed into the wet pulp. Pulped construction paper adds flecks of color to paper, but the colors are not lightfast and the quality of the paper is not high.

Dried flowers and leaves

Dried flowers and leaves add a special dimension and color to handmade paper. Flowers with light, delicate petals, such as pansies, violas and hydrangea, press easily and dry quickly. If you'd like to add the petals of heavier flowers, such as sunflowers, roses or daisies, to your handmade paper, prepare them by gently tearing the petals away from the calyx before pressing. Choose thin leaves, such as those from hardwood or lemon trees, to add to paper. Thick, fibrous leaves, such as rubber tree or begonia leaves, will not dry well.

Press leaves, delicate flowers or petals between sheets of newspaper under heavy books until they are dry, which takes at least two or three days. Make sure they are completely dry before adding them to the paper to prevent the growth of mold in the finished paper.

To incorporate the dried flowers, petals or leaves into the paper, add them to the pulpy water in your vat just before forming the sheet of paper, as described on page 38.

Threads

Snip threads or strings of any color or material you like into short or long pieces, from ½ inch (1 cm) to 4 inches (10 cm). You can add short snips of thread to the pulpy water before forming sheets of paper, as described on page 38. Alternately, short or long threads can be added to a wet sheet of paper after you have rolled it off the mold and onto the felt. Simply lay or sprinkle the threads on the wet sheet. Press it as usual and the threads will become embedded in the paper.

Vegetable fibers

The threads of celery, rhubarb, asparagus and other fibrous vegetables, can be added to hand-made paper. The vegetable threads add a hint of color and swirly texture to your paper.

To prepare the vegetables, cut them into 2 inch (5 cm) pieces, then cover with water and simmer for several hours (add water as needed to keep them covered) until the vegetables are very mushy. Under running water, mash the vegetables between your fingers to separate the long fibers. Then rub the threads in a fine sieve to be sure they are free of soft clinging tissue.

Add the vegetable fibers to your vat of pulpy water just before forming sheets of paper (see page 38).

Making Paper

Equipment

- two rust-proof pails

- plastic or rust-proof fine sieve

- deckle and mold: frames for forming sheets (purchase a set from a craft or specialty store or make them according to instructions that follow)

- vat: dishpan or laundry tub at least 10 inches (25 cm) deep and 8 inches (20 cm) larger in width and length than the deckle-and-mold outside dimensions

- household blender

- sponges

- old blanket or towels

- "felts": interfacing fabric (not the iron-on type), wool felt or tightly woven linen or cotton fabric cut about 4 inches (10 cm) larger in width and length than the deckle and mold (the paper will have the same texture as the felts)

- pressing boards: sheets of wood, baking sheets or heavy cutting boards piled with books, or make a press with two sheets of 16 × 20 inches (40 cm × 50 cm) plywood and clamps

- large sheet of formica, glass, or acrylic for drying sheets (optional)

- rolling pin or brayer (optional)

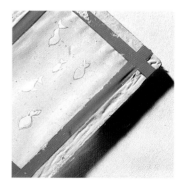

Making a Deckle and Mold

The mold is the mesh-covered frame that forms the sheet of paper; the deckle is the open frame that contains the edges of the paper. A versatile size for paper, and a frame size that is easy to work with, is an inside dimension of 6 × 8 inches (15 cm × 20 cm).

Equipment

- $\frac{3}{8} \times \frac{3}{8}$ inch (9 mm $\times$ 9 mm) sections of wood–teak, mahogany or any hardwood that is not knotted or twisted; four cut $8\frac{3}{4}$ inches (22 cm) long and four cut 6 inches (15 cm) long for a deckle and mold that will make 6 $\times$ 8 inch (15 cm $\times$ 20 cm) paper

- water-proof wood glue

- 16 brass L-shaped, screw-in corner braces to hold the wood together

- brass or aluminum screen mesh with 30 to 65 wires per inch (2.5 cm) or fine textured nylon netting

- rust-proof staples or brass tacks

To make a deckle and mold

To make the mold, put two of the $8\frac{3}{4}$ inch (22 cm) wood sections on a work table; place two of the 6" (15 cm) sections perpendicular to the longer sections, at the top and bottom to form a frame. Apply waterproof wood glue at the joints and allow to dry. Secure the four sections together at the corners with the L-shaped braces.

Fold under the edges of the screen so the wires don't scratch your fingers. Stretch the piece of screen mesh over the frame and secure the screen to the frame with staples or tacks. If you're using nylon netting, thoroughly wet the netting before stretching it tightly across the frame.

Make the deckle in the same manner, except do not put screen on the deckle.

Papermaking materials

- paper for pulping (see "Quality In–Quality Out" on page 21)

- dyes for coloring paper, including paper napkins, crepe paper, food coloring, onion skins, powdered turmeric (a spice), strong-brewed coffee or tea; see page 33 (optional)

- additions to paper, including dried flowers and leaves, celery fibers, pine needles, confetti, glitter, or snips of thread, fabric or paper; see page 25 (optional)

- gelatin or liquid laundry starch to size the paper: use if you plan to draw or paint on the paper; see page 35 (optional)

Tear threads from lossely woven fabric to add to paper.

To make paper

- At least one day before papermaking, tear your paper for pulping into stamp-size pieces. Tear rather than cut the paper because the torn edges can better absorb water. An exception: if you have access to a paper shredding machine, shredded paper works very well.

- The amount of paper you tear depends on how much paper you want to make. The amount of paper you make will be about 75% of the amount you have torn up. In other words, if you tear 12 sheets

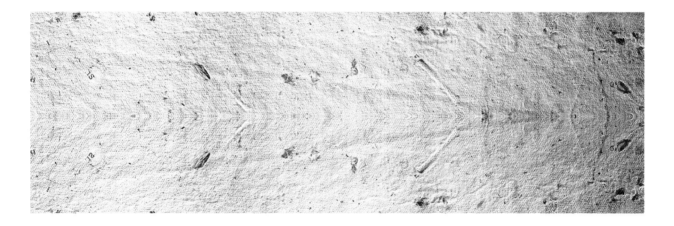

of standard size personal stationery, you will probably have enough pulp to make 9 sheets of 6 × 8 inch (15 cm × 20 cm) paper.

- Put the torn paper in a plastic pail and cover it with cool water. Stir it with your hands to make sure all the paper has contact with water. Let the paper soak for at least 12 hours. When the paper has soaked sufficiently, it will be very fragile.

- Assemble all the equipment and soaked paper in an area where you have running water and a drain where splashes won't damage anything. Always strain pulp through a sieve; never allow pulp or paper to go down a drain because it will cause a clog.

- Make sure your blender has no grease or food particles in it before pulping the paper. Put a fistful (about $\frac{1}{2}$ cup) of soaked paper in the clean blender and fill the blender with cool water. Turn the blender to low then to high (this is easier on the blender's motor) and whirl the paper for 15 seconds. Check the consistency of the pulp. It should look creamy. A good way to be sure it has been pulped

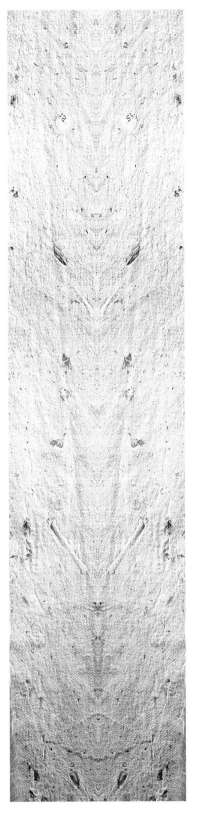

sufficiently is to pour a small amount of pulp into a clear jar of water and hold it up to a strong light. If there are floating chunks of unpulped paper, whirl the pulp for another 10 seconds and check it again. (Heavy papers will take longer to break down.)

- Pour the pulp from the blender into a pail or large bowl. Continue to blend the soaked paper until it is all pulped. As you go, drain some of the water by pouring the watery pulp through a fine sieve. Leave enough water in the pail to cover the pulp.

If you are not going to use the pulp to make paper immediately, prevent souring by adding 2 drops of household bleach to one gallon of pulp and mix well; drain off most of the water through a fine, rust-proof sieve. You can store the drained pulp in a covered container or zip top freezer bag in the refrigerator for up to one month or in the freezer indefinitely.

Adding cotton linter

Tear sheets of cotton linter (see page 24) into stamp-size pieces and soak in cool water for at least 10 minutes. If the linter is already shredded, simply soak it. Pulp in a blender as you did the paper. Add to the pail of pulp and blend well with your hand.

Dyeing pulp

If you want to color all or part of the pulp, now is the time to add a coloring agent. Before adding the dye, pour the pulp-water mixture through a fine sieve until the pulp is thick but still wet.

The pulp will be cloud-like—very soft to the touch, fluffy and a bit runny. If you remove too much of the water and the pulp is stiff, just add more water.

The amounts and ratios of coloring agents and pulp given below are only guidelines for your projects. Remember that regardless of the type of dye you use, the color of the dyed paper lightens considerably as the paper dries.

Most of the dyes that color paper will also stain your clothing and some will stain your hands, so be sure to wear a smock or old shirt when working with dyes. Rubber gloves will protect your hands from stains. (None of the dyeing agents mentioned here is a health risk.) You may like more or less color depending on the purpose for your paper.

• To dye pulp with colored paper napkins, tissue or crepe paper, tear the colored paper into very small pieces and pulp thoroughly as above. The water will be deeply colored. Combine the colored water and pulp with the plain pulp in a large jar or zip top freezer bag. Store in the refrigerator overnight to allow the plain pulp to absorb dye.

There are many ways to dye pulp – remember that shades will inevitably lighten as the paper dries. Clockwise from top center: food coloring colors paper a pastel shade; strong tea dyes paper off-white; a measuring cup is filled with pulp that was dyed with turmeric, a common spice; powdered coffee dyes paper off-white to light brown, depending on the strength of the solution; boil onion skins in water and use the colored water to dye paper light tan; turmeric is a spice also used to dye fabric and colors paper a vivid gold.

- To dye pulp with turmeric, which will make the paper golden yellow, mix ¼ cup powdered turmeric in 1 cup water. Add the mixture to 1 gallon (5 L) of pulp and mix well. Pour into a large jar or zip-top freezer bag. Store in the refrigerator overnight to allow the plain pulp to absorb the dye.

- To dye pulp with onion skins, which will make the paper light tan, simmer 2 cups of dry onion skins (loosely packed) in a medium saucepan in water to cover for one hour or until the skins are light in color and the water is brown. If you want to use only the dye-water, drain the onion skins in a sieve, discard the skins and add the dye water to 2 quarts (3 L) of pulp. If you want to use the dye-water and skins in the paper, let the skins and water cool completely, then puree in a blender until the skins are small flecks (or large flecks, if you like). Then, add the skins and water to 2 quarts (3 L) of pulp. Pour into a large jar or zip-top freezer bag. Store in the refrigerator overnight to allow the plain pulp to absorb dye.

- To dye pulp with food coloring, which will make the paper a pastel version of the color you choose, pour ¼ cup liquid food coloring into 2 quarts (3 L) of pulp; mix well with a wooden spoon. Pour into a large jar or zip-top freezer bag. Store in the refrigerator overnight to allow the plain pulp to absorb dye.

- To dye pulp with coffee or tea, which will make the paper light golden brown, make strong coffee (add approximately 4 teaspoons of dry, instant coffee to 1 cup of boiling water) or brew tea (4 tea bags to 1 cup of boiling water). Dilute the hot coffee or tea with one cup of cold water, then pour it into 2 quarts (3 L) of pulp. Pour into a large jar or zip-top freezer bag. Store in the refrigerator overnight to allow the plain pulp to absorb dye.

Vat-sizing paper

Vat-sizing incorporates size into the fibers of the paper. Sizing–whether in the vat or after the paper is made–prevents paint or ink from running along the fibers, making spidery lines in your handmade paper. You can vat-size with gelatin or liquid laundry starch.

To use gelatin, dissolve half a packet of plain gelatin in ¼ cup of warm water, then mix it into the water in your vat (about 2 gallons or 12 L of water.)

To use laundry starch, mix one tablespoon in ¼ cup of warm water, then mix this into the water in your vat (about 2 gallons or 12 L of water.)

Threads frayed from fabric or from a spool can be added to pulp to become a decorative and strengthening addition to paper.

Forming sheets of paper

Before forming a sheet of paper, prepare a "couching" area. This is where you will stack your wet sheets to be pressed before drying. Put one pressing board in an area near the vat where water won't cause damage. If the pressing boards are not laminated with formica or melamine put a sheet of plastic on top of the board to prevent warping. Thoroughly wet the felts and put one felt on the pressing board.

Fill your vat halfway with water. Add about 1 cup of partially drained pulp and mix it well with your hand. Mix the pulp frequently as you work, because it sinks fast. After you make each sheet of paper, replace some pulp for the next sheet. As you gain experience, you will learn to know when the water/pulp ratio is right and how to make sheets that are as thick or thin as you like.

Make a few sheets of plain paper for practice before adding things to your paper. If you're adding leaves, flowers or other things, like glitter or threads, now is the time to add them (see page 25.) Simply put the items you're adding in the pulpy water and they will become part of the paper. Use your judgment as to the amounts of things you add. (Dried flowers and leaves tend to gather around the outside of the vat, so you may find you catch only a few in the mold.)

A sheet of newly formed paper, above, still on the frame with the deckle askew, is ready to be rolled onto a felt.

Save dried flowers, left, to add to paper. Some flowers "bleed," making streaks and blobs of color on the finished sheets. A remedy is to let the dried flowers soak in warm water for 20 minutes before adding the flowers to the pulp.

To form a sheet of paper, hold the deckle and mold together with the deckle on top and the screen side of the mold up. In other words, make a sandwich with the screen in the center.

In one smooth, continuous motion:

- dip the mold deep into the pulpy water vertically with the side farthest away from you going in first;

- continue to push the mold until it is horizontal;

- quickly pull the mold straight up–still horizontal–out of the pulpy water;

- while the pulp is still very watery, give the mold a quick shake side to side and back and forth, which is called "throwing off the wave" because the pulp looks and sounds like an ocean wave, and this action helps the fibers interlock;

- tip the mold at a slight angle to let excess water drain off into the vat for 20 seconds;

- place the deckle and mold on a flat surface and carefully remove the deckle so that no water drips onto the sheet which would make holes (these are called "papermakers' tears.")

If for any reason you do not like the sheet you've made (too thin, thick or uneven) simply dip the mold back into the vat and the pulp will easily float back into the water.

1

2

The steps for making handmade paper.

1. Fill a vat about half full with water and add prepared pulp; hold your deckle and mold firmly together, then in one smooth motion, push the deckle and mold into the pulpy water and lift it straight up, giving it a quick shake front to back and side to side; then remove the deckle carefully to avoid dripping water onto the wet sheet and let the water drain off for about 20 seconds.

2. Have a stack of damp newspapers and a wet "felt" ready to receive a sheet of wet paper; rest the edge of the mold on the felt and gently roll it face-down onto the felt; sponge the back of the mold through the mesh to absorb excess water.

3. Carefully pull the mold away from the wet sheet. Place another wet felt over the wet sheet to prepare for the next sheet. A stack of wet sheets of paper is called a post.

3

4

5

4. You can press your post of paper between sheets of plywood or laminated wood. Here, the plywood is protected from water with sheets of white plastic. The post of paper is placed between the boards, then clamps are tightened to squeeze out water and to strengthen the paper.

5. Still on their felts, damp sheets of paper are placed on newspaper to dry. Paper dries more quickly if a fan is directed to blow just above the paper and dries very quickly when left in the sun. For paper with one very smooth side, place the paper with its felt (paper-side down) on a sheet of glass or acrylic, roll lightly with a rolling pin and leave to dry. Regardless of the method of drying, remove the sheets from their felts when they are nearly or completely dry. The paper will probably be wavy. If you want it to lie flat, you can weight a stack of paper under heavy books for a few days or lightly press one sheet at a time with a warm iron.

Making a "post" or stack of paper

- Take the pulp-covered mold to the pressing board. Place one long side of the mold on one edge of the wet felt and, in one smooth motion, roll the mold onto the felt until the wet sheet and mold are lying on the felt.

- With a sponge, gently blot excess water from the back of the screen.

- Slowly and carefully pull the deckle and screen away from the wet sheet of paper.

- Place another wet felt over the wet sheet of paper.

- Continue adding sheets and felts to the post in this way.

A stack of wet sheets of paper, still attached to their felts, is called a "post" of paper.

Press a post of newly formed paper between plastic-covered plywood and apply pressure with clamps to remove excess water and to strengthen the paper.

Pressing the post

Press the post outside or in the floor of a shower or bathtub, because a lot of water will escape from the post as it's pressed.

Cover the top sheet of paper with plastic, if necessary, to protect the top pressing board from water. Attach the clamps to the corners of the pressing boards, and turn the clamp screws to apply pressure to the post.

If you're not using pressing boards and clamps, put a baking sheet or sheet of wood on top of the post and stack books on top. For a quick squeeze, stand on the top board for a minute, then stack books or bricks on top.

Pressure squeezes out excess water and, more importantly, makes the paper stronger by helping the fibers interweave. Leave the post under weight or pressure for at least one hour and up to 24 hours.

Drying the paper

Remove the weights or clamps from the pressing boards. Very carefully–to avoid tearing the wet paper–separate the sheets with their felts still attached. Do not try to separate the sheets and felts at this point.

Place the sheets of paper and felts on a flat, newspaper-covered area to dry. Or, you can hang the felts with paper attached on an indoor clothesline.

On dry, sunny days, you can spread your paper out on the grass or on a blanket to dry in the sun.

If you want very smooth sheets, dry them on glass or formica. Simply place the paper and felt (paper side down) on the smooth surface. Gently and lightly roll the paper flat against the surface with a rolling pin or brayer. Leave the felt on the paper until dry.

Whichever indoor drying method you use, you will find that a fan gently blowing just over the surface of the wet paper will help it dry much faster.

Drying will take several hours or overnight. When the sheets are dry to the touch, gently peel the paper from the felts.

Unless dried on flat surfaces, the sheets will most likely be wavy. If you want them to be flatter, place a stack of dry paper under heavy books for several days. Or, you can press them on a hard surface with a medium-hot iron. Do not press hard or you will make an impression of the flat of the iron in the paper.

External sizing

If you didn't vat-size and would like to use your paper for writing, drawing or painting, you can size externally. There are some advantages to external size. The size may be more evenly applied and may make the paper stronger.

You can use gelatin or starch by spraying or dipping for external sizing. Either way, let your paper age for at least three weeks or it may disintegrate during the sizing process.

The simplest and quickest way to externally size paper is to spray on size, using spray-on laundry starch. Place the paper on a sheet of newspaper and spray it evenly with spray starch. With a medium-hot iron, lightly press until dry.

To dip in starch or gelatin, first dissolve one tablespoon liquid laundry starch in $\frac{1}{4}$ cup hot water; or, dissolve $\frac{1}{2}$ packet plain gelatin in $\frac{1}{4}$ cup hot water. Add either starch or gelatin to one gallon (6 L) hot water in a shallow pan and mix well.

Slip the paper into the size and leave a few seconds until the paper has absorbed the size. Gently pull the paper out of the pan. Place the wet paper between two dry felts and gently press with a rolling pin or brayer to remove air bubbles. Dry the paper using any of the methods described under "Drying the paper."

Decorating ■ Paper

3

Decorating paper is a fun and creative way to add new life to old or plain paper. You can use most of the decorating methods in this chapter to give lively interest to drawing, newsprint, watercolor, tissue, computer, typing, wallpaper, kraft and handmade papers.

Choose the weight and quality of the paper you decorate according to how you will use the final product. For example, if you're decorating paper with tempera paint and a block printer to be used for gift wrap, you can use a lightweight, low-quality paper like newsprint, typing or kraft. On the other hand, if you're stenciling a paper with oil paint to use to cover a frame that will hold a treasured family photograph, you'll want a good-quality paper like a high-rag, acid-free drawing, handmade or watercolor paper.

Basic supplies

• paper for decorating: choose the weight and quality of the paper according to the decorating method and the use you have in mind for the decorated paper (suggestions are made in the instructions for each method)

• extra paper for testing

• newspapers to protect surfaces

• a smock or old shirt to wear to protect your clothing from paint and wax

Additional supplies needed for specific projects are listed with each method.

From the free-form
of spattering and
dribbling to the
careful application
of block prints,
decorating paper is
fun, easy and often
quick.

You can make block prints by dipping various items into paint or ink. Experiment with vegetables, natural sponges, Styrofoam, cookie cutters, forks, manufactured sponges, leaves, keys, and rubber erasers.

Block Printing

Block printing is an easy way to make gorgeous abstract or representational designs. Once the block is found or made, applying the design is simple; just dip the block in paint or press onto an ink pad and stamp it on paper.

You can have fun experimenting with various effects with block prints and can use block-printed paper in many ways—gift wrap, note cards, frames, boxes or book covers. The paper you decorate with block printing can be white, black or any color in between. You can also get unusual effects by block printing over paper that has a pre-printed design on it.

You don't have to cut blocks for printing—you can use existing objects, such as forks, corks or jar lids. If you're going to cut a design out of wax, soap, an eraser or a root vegetable, remember that bold, large designs will be easier to cut than thin, spindly shapes.

Right, a spiral was cut from cardboard, glued onto a round of cardboard, then painted with white glue to protect it from warping.

Block prints can be made by cutting Styrofoam into shapes, then gluing the shapes onto another piece of Styrofoam or cardboard, as at right.

Equipment

• basic supplies listed on page 46

• objects for making the blocks:

For permanent, reusable blocks, try any of the following: paraffin wax bars, flat bars of soap, manufactured sponges (the very thin kind that expand in water are easiest to cut), rubber erasers, wooden dowels, forks, water glasses, thick or corrugated cardboard, Styrofoam (from packed meat or disposable plates), wood blocks, natural sponges, a cookie cutter or a potato masher

For temporary, short-life blocks, try any of these: strong, fresh leaves (azalea, lemon or ivy leaves or pine needles) or root vegetables (potato, turnip or carrot)

• craft knife for cutting the blocks (optional)

• paint: watercolor, tempera, acrylic or oil paint, or a rubber stamp ink pad

• stack of plates or paper plates covered with wet paper towels to hold paint

To block print

First, decide on a design, considering how it will look as a repeat across and up and down the paper. You can make some designs that will "float" on the paper with space around them. And some designs will be stamped onto paper very close together to create a continuous flow of design.

Also consider the size of the paper to be decorated. Large sheets of gift wrap, for example, can take a large design (or a smaller design can be stamped on with many repeats or lots of space around each design imprint). If the decorated paper will be used to cover a pocket-size sketch book, for example, the design repeats will need to be small, or only part of a large design will show, which is an artistic decision you can make.

Make a colorful, bold design with a large plastic salad fork dipped in two colors of paint.

Red and blue eight-pointed stars were stamped on paper with a block made from cardboard shapes glued onto a cardboard base. Gold flowers were also stamped from cardboard cutouts; blue stars from a cookie cutter, and blue boys and girls from manufactured sponges.

Make the block

To make a block from paraffin wax, soap, rubber erasers or root vegetables:

- Draw your design idea on a piece of paper, or if you're copying a design you like from a book, magazine or other source, follow any of the Design Transfer Techniques described on page 13.

- Keep in mind that some block print designs are "positive" and some are "negative." In other words, the part of the block you cut away will show as white on the paper and the part you leave will show as color. So, you can cut away the background–for a "positive" print–or leave the background and cut away the design–for a "negative" print.

- Draw or transfer the design onto the wax or eraser with a pencil. For root vegetables, cut the vegetable in half and dry the surface well with paper towels before transferring the design.

Both cat designs were cut from rubber erasers. The cat on the left is "negative" and the cat on the right is "positive." You can see on the paper how each stamp prints.

For a "positive" image:

- With a craft knife, cut straight down around the pencil marks. Then, with the knife held at an angle, carefully cut away the background at least $\frac{1}{4}$ - $\frac{3}{8}$ inch (6-9 mm) deep, leaving the design intact.

For a "negative" image:

- With a craft knife, cut straight down around the pencil marks, then with the knife held at an angle, carefully cut out the design area.

To make a block from a manufactured sponge, cardboard or Styrofoam:

• Draw the design onto the sponge, cardboard or Styrofoam with a pencil.

• With scissors or a craft knife, cut out the design.

  Note: if the cardboard you are using is not thick enough to withstand repeated stamping, you can glue the cut out design to a block of corrugated cardboard or Styrofoam.

To make cardboard water-resistant for repeated use, rub it well with solid floor wax (butcher's wax) or spray it with spray-on furniture wax, and let it stand for 15 minutes before rubbing off the excess with absorbent paper.

To use existing items, like natural sponges, corks, wooden dowels, a potato masher, a water glass or leaves as block printers, no special preparation is needed.

Bold designs are simple to make with a cut potato or the bottom of a water glass dipped onto a paint-soaked sponge, then pressed onto paper.

Block print with an ink pad

Ink pads made for rubber stamps are available in art and office supply stores in many sizes and colors—including metallic and rainbow colors. You can use a well-inked

Sponges that are packaged flat and thin and then expand in water are easy to cut into shapes.

ink pad to print with materials that have some "tooth" to grip and hold the ink: wood, rubber erasers, natural or manufactured sponges and root vegetables. Or experiment with smoother objects such as glass, plastic, metal and leaves for special effects.

You can use ink to make very effective designs on any weight or quality of paper. Because the ink from an ink pad is relatively dry, you can use it on thin paper, like tissue paper, without causing the paper to shrink and buckle when the ink dries.

53

To print with an ink pad

- Simply stamp the block on the ink pad and then onto paper.

- Test your block on a piece of scrap paper similar to the paper you will be decorating.

Block printing with paint

Use a block–one you've carved or an existing shape made of any material–on any weight or quality of paper. Water-based paints will not stick to paraffin wax, so use acrylic or oil paint to print with a wax bar.

Various combinations of weights and qualities of paper with different kinds of paint will give you very different results. For example, very wet paint will make thin paper buckle when the paint dries, creating an interesting texture on the finished decorated paper, which you can use as gift wrap or to stuff a paper bag that holds a gift. If you don't want a buckled paper, use heavy paper or a paint with an oil or acrylic base or mix tempera paint so it is thick. Keep in mind, also, that the color of water-based paint tends to lighten a bit as it dries. Test your

An apple cut in half and dipped in metallic acrylic paint makes an elegant design repeated on yellow paper, at left.

Above, trailing gold flowers and gold and blue spirals were printed with shapes cut from cardboard glued onto cardboard bases. Blue star shapes were stamped with a cookie cutter, then highlighted with gold dribbles. Carefully cut from flat sponges, girl and boy shapes were printed to hold hands in rows.

paint on paper and let it dry to check the shade before you apply paint to the paper to be decorated.

To print with paint

- Mix paint, if necessary, to the thickness you desire, according to directions on the package.

- Pour a small amount of paint onto a paper plate, so the paint makes a shallow pool. (Acrylic paint tends to dry quickly, so you can extend its usefulness by pouring the paint onto wet paper towels which are on a plate for support.)

- Stamp your block into the paint, making sure the block is evenly covered.

- Test your block and paint on a scrap of paper before you apply paint to the paper to be decorated. Let the paint dry to check the shade of the paint and the effect the paint has on the paper.

- Then, stamp the paint-covered block onto paper to be decorated.

Have fun with block printing by experimenting with the following options, or create your own new techniques.

Use the same shape in two or more different colors:

- Cover the paper as desired with one color, leaving some empty spaces between the shapes, if you like; let the paint or ink dry.

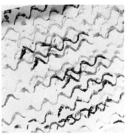

- Dip the clean shape in a different color of paint or ink pad and apply the new color in empty spaces between the first application or on top of the shapes on the paper.

Edges of cardboard–plain or corrugated–can be dipped in paint and used to print designs on paper. Or, use your fingertips to create birds, fish or flowers, as shown on this page and at left.

Use more than one shape on the same paper:

- Choose the shapes that you want to use and apply one shape onto paper with paint or ink, leaving space for the next shape, if desired; let the paint or ink dry.

- Apply the next shape with the same or different color of paint or ink in empty spaces or directly over the shapes on the paper.

Use two or more transparent colors in the same or combinations of shapes:

- Mix very light colors with liquid watercolor paint so the paint is nearly transparent when it dries.

- Stamp the same or a different shape in a different color over the shapes on the paper.

Use your hands as blocks for printing:

- Dip a part of your hand in paint or ink. Try using fingertips, the pad of your thumb, palms, fingernails or sides of your hands. Does a fingerprint look like the center of a flower? Use a pen or colored pencil to add  flower petals. Or add details to bring out images of animal faces, falling leaves, swimming fish or other images that you see in the designs.

Use the edges of cardboard to make designs:

- Cut rectangles or squares in any length from flat or corrugated cardboard. Dip one edge of the cardboard into paint or ink and stamp straight or curved shapes onto paper. With a clean piece of cardboard, repeat the stamping in a different color, if you like.

Fresh, stiff leaves can be used as blocks to print on envelopes, as above, or on many other paper items, including gift wrap.

- Then, if you want to, you can fill in the design with dots, hearts, flowers or any other shape you like with paint, pen or colored pencils.

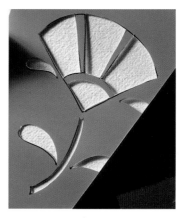

Stencils can be cut from thin, stiff cardboard or, for a stencil with a longer life, from acetate. The small thistle stencil, above, is cut from cardboard. Once a stencil is cut, you can use it to decorate gift wrap, book covers, wallpaper, greeting cards, or box lids.

Stencils

Stenciling, like block printing, is a repetitive design technique that you can use to cover paper thoroughly with beautiful designs, or make borders or designs with lots of space around them.

You can buy pre-cut stencils in craft and home-decorating stores, or you can cut your own. Many pre-cut stencils are wistful, old-fashioned designs, such as marching geese, hearts, flowers and ribbon swags. Depending on your taste and the style of the finished decorated paper you want, you can purchase these stencils or copy designs from books, magazines or other sources (see Design Transfer Techniques on page 13).

Or make your own abstract or representational designs with stencils in any size, according to the size of the paper you're decorating.

Choose the paper you will stencil according to the use you have in mind for the decorated paper. Use handmade, typing, computer or notebook paper for small designs and use to wrap small gifts, for making holiday ornaments or greeting cards. For some projects, you can stencil the backs of used paper.

Large sheets of kraft, drawing, watercolor or tracing paper can be stenciled with large or small designs. (For very ambitious stenciling, you can make continuous designs on rolls of kraft paper.) Use these for gift wrap, to cover frames, books, portfolios or boxes—maybe even for wallpaper for a small room or closet!

The large Caribbean leaf and Christmas ball designs, above, are both cut from acetate and can be used many times.

Equipment

- basic supplies listed on page 46

- purchased stencils (optional)

- to make stencils: thin cardboard (for short-term projects) or acetate sheets (acetate can be used many times without wearing)

- to mark designs on cardboard: pencil or other method according to instructions in Design Transfer Techniques on page 13; to mark designs on acetate: permanent felt-tip marker or wax china marker

- craft knife

- paint: watercolor, tempera or acrylic

- stencil brushes with short, stiff bristles—one brush for each color of paint used

- stack of plates or paper plates covered with wet paper towels for holding paint

Note: To make cardboard water-resistant for repeated use, rub it well with solid floor wax or spray it with spray-on furniture wax; let it stand for 15 minutes before rubbing off the excess with absorbent paper.

Fantasy flowers cut from acetate, left, are ready to be stenciled onto a greeting card.

To cut and use a stencil

- Draw your design idea on paper, remembering: that only the cut-out spaces will carry the colors of paint when the stencil is used, you can use as many different colors as you like for your design, and all the parts of the design that are not cut out must be attached to the body of the stencil.

- You can copy designs from any source and transfer them according to instructions in Design Transfer Techniques on page 13.

- To cut a stencil from cardboard or acetate: draw or transfer your design onto thin cardboard with pencil, felt-tip marker or china marker, or other technique; then, with a craft knife, carefully cut out the parts of the design that will be painted.

- Mix paint, if necessary, according to directions on package.

- Pour a small amount of paint on paper plates or wet paper towels.

- Dab the paintbrush into the paint with the bristles pointed straight down, until the brush is lightly coated with paint. Do not overload the brush with paint or the paint will smear when you pull up the stencil.

- Try the stencil on scrap paper to test the stencil and paint.

- With the bristles of the brush pointed straight down, dab the paint into the spaces cut out of the stencil, beginning

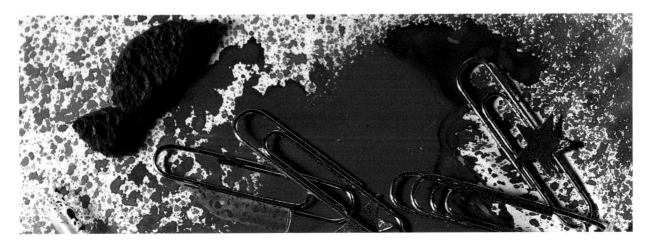

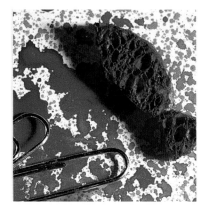

around the edges of the cut-out areas, then filling in the centers. If you're using more than one color of paint, use a clean brush and dab in additional paints in the appropriate areas, being careful as you dab that paints of different colors don't overlap into other areas.

- Carefully lift the stencil from the paper.

- Repeat this process on the paper to be decorated as many times as necessary to cover the paper as you like it.

Spattering, Spraying, Dribbling

Spattering, spraying and dribbling are methods for covering paper with paint very quickly. Children really enjoy these techniques, and there are no "wrong" results. Be sure to cover all vulnerable surfaces, including the floor, with newspaper, cover yourself and the children with smocks, then spread out large or small sheets of paper and get started!

You can use these techniques to decorate poster board, paper plates (for crafts, but not for carrying food), newsprint, paper towels, drawing paper, tissue or tracing paper (for a puckered finish when the paint dries), computer, notebook, typing or gift-wrap paper.

Use the decorated paper for making greeting cards, holiday ornaments, masks, table place cards, gift tags or gift wrap, or to cover plant pots, picture frames, portfolios, books, boxes, vases, bowls or trays.

Equipment

- basic supplies listed on page 46

- tempera paint in several colors, mixed thin or thick, according to the results you want

- for spattering: old toothbrushes, paintbrushes and small pieces of cardboard, or towels or sheets torn into large squares

- for spraying: household spray bottles, such as misters for plants

- for dribbling: old measuring cups, spoons, clean milk cartons, or anything that will hold small amounts of paint

You can use leaves, as shown at right, as a resist when you spray paper with paint. From top to bottom, lay leaves on the paper; spray paint from a water bottle; remove the leaves. Try this technique with palm fronds, pine needles or daisy petals.

Spattering and dribbling

- To spatter: pour paint into jars; dip brushes into paint, then quickly run your finger or a piece of cardboard across the bristles to spatter paint onto the paper; or dip wads of damp towels or sheets into paint, then sling the paint onto the paper.

- To spray: pour paint into spray bottles and spray paint onto the paper. Adjust the nozzle of the spray bottle to get a light mist or a direct, hard spray.

- To dribble: pour paint into a container and dribble paint onto the paper in circles, zigzags or other designs.

Have fun with spattering, spraying and dribbling by experimenting with the following options—or come up with your own new techniques:

- Use two or more colors of paint for any of these methods; apply one color, let it dry, then apply another.

- If you want the designs you make to stay in dots and dribbles, lay the papers out flat on the floor or table until the paint is dry; if you want a drippy (Jackson Pollock) look, prop the papers up on an easel.

- Dampen the papers with a sponge before applying paint. The paint will bleed and run on the wet paper.

- Mask parts of the paper with tape or shapes of cardboard or paper. Let the first application of paint dry, remove the masks, then apply another color of paint.

Snips of triangular-shaped magazine paper were scattered over white paper, which was then sprayed with dilute blue acrylic paint, giving the decorated paper a nautical, sail- boat theme when the snips were removed.

There are several interesting ways you can use crayons to decorate paper. You can draw designs then press the paper with a warm iron, which melts the wax and sets it into the paper. The resulting paper has a waxy, flexible texture.

Or, try melting crayons in either of the two ways described below and drip or apply the hot wax onto the paper with a knife.

Note: Young children can make designs that an adult then irons, but children should never be involved in working with hot, melted crayons–hot wax is flammable and can cause severe burns to skin.

Crayons

Crayons–inexpensive, readily available and easy to use–can be employed in sophisticated ways when you think of them as colored wax rather than as children's playthings. Once crayons are applied to paper in any of the following ways, the colors are permanent and will never fade.

Decorate any weight or quality of paper with crayons–depending on your use for the finished paper. You can use small sheets of notebook, typing or computer paper for short-lived paper projects, like gift wrap, gift tags or party hats or masks. Or, use good quality, acid-free handmade, drawing, tracing or computer paper for projects that will have long lives: covering books, vases, trays, frames and boxes, or making holiday ornaments, note paper or greeting cards.

Equipment

- basic supplies listed on page 46

- crayons–new or stubs–with papers removed

- for ironing design into paper: electric iron and waste paper for covering the design before ironing (Note: the ink from newspaper or slick magazine pages will transfer to the design, which can add an attractive scruffy element; or use unprinted newsprint or other inexpensive paper.)

Crayons give vivid, long-lasting color to decorating projects. At left, crayons are melted in cupcake papers and kept warm over hot water, then used to block print on paper. Above, crayons were used to draw a design and message on paper. Crayon resisted a coat of brown water-based paint.

- for decorating paper with melted crayons: an electric hot plate or candle, old cans for melting crayons, and old spoons or knives or other flat objects for applying the hot wax

- oven mits or pads to protect your hands from heat

To heat-set a crayon design

- Make a design in any number of crayon colors on paper. Put a sheet of plain or printed waste paper over the design, then press a warm iron on the waste paper with an up and down motion. (Newsprint will sometimes leave some of its ink on your design. Iron the newspaper to prevent this.) Remove the waste paper and check the appearance of the design. If the crayon hasn't melted sufficiently, apply clean waste paper and iron again.

To decorate paper with melted crayons

- Put crayons in old cans or cupcake papers. Melt crayons of similar colors together. Mix carefully, because if you use crayons in the red, blue and yellow families together, you'll end up with a batch of brown. Put the can into a pan of hot water over heat on a stove or hot plate and stir until the crayons are melted.

Caution: Melted wax is flammable and dangerous. Handle with care! Dribble the hot colored wax from the can to paper with an old spoon or dip a knife or cotton swab into the wax and apply the wax to the paper.

- Light a fat candle and hold a knife or other flat object over the flame until the knife is hot (this happens very quickly); rub a crayon on the hot knife until you have a small pool of melted wax, then flatten the knife, with the hot wax down, onto paper. You can also use a spoon for melting the wax over the flame, then dribble wax onto the paper quickly before the melted crayon hardens.

The design opposite was applied by melting crayons on a knife over a flame, then flattening the knife on paper.

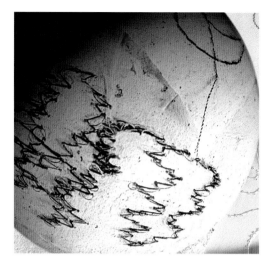

Sewing by Hand or Machine

Sew designs onto paper with embroidery stitches, zigzags or simple running stitches by hand or with a sewing machine. You can also "applique" pieces of ribbon, cutouts of paper or fabric, or snips of foil onto paper. Using string or embroidery floss, you can sew the edges of paper together to form an envelope.

Paper decorated by sewing is most useful for notepaper and greeting cards, as well as book covers, boxes, books, picture frames and mats.

Equipment

- basic supplies listed on page 46

- sewing machine (optional)

- sewing needle (optional)

- threads in various colors and weights

To sew on paper

- If you're using a sewing machine: thread the machine with the color and weight of thread you like. If your machine makes fancy or zigzag stitches, experiment with them on scrap paper. (Sewing through paper dulls needles, so remove and replace the needle you use with a fresh needle before sewing fabric.)

- If you're sewing the paper by hand, thread a needle with the color and weight of thread you like. Some stitches are better than others on paper–stitches that are very close together will perforate the paper and tear it. Experiment with stitches on scrap paper.

Free-form or controlled, straight or zigzag machine stitches decorate paper quickly and easily. A sample of hand-sewn paper can be seen at the lower left of the photograph at right.

Batik on paper is a many-stepped project involving painting the paper with melted wax, then paint, and repeating the process several times until the design is completed. A dark, abstract batik design on brown kraft paper is shown above. The paper was used to cover a portfolio, shown on page 97.

Batik or Wax-Resist

Beautifully decorated fabrics are made using the batik method with wax and fabric dyes. Similar methods can also be used to decorate paper. The idea is to apply wax-resist to the paper, so the areas covered with wax remain the color under the wax, while the rest of the paper absorbs a new color.

You can dip objects, such as cookie cutters, into hot wax or liquid floor wax, then apply the wax to paper. (Read the section about block printing beginning on page 49, and use the same types of objects and methods to apply wax resist to paper for batiking. Do not dip your fingers or hand into hot wax.) Or you can paint the wax onto paper with a brush or dribble it on with a spoon.

Young children can make designs with floor wax, but children should never be involved in working with hot, melted paraffin or crayons—hot wax is flammable and can cause severe burns to skin.

Use heavy, good-quality papers for this method because you'll be applying at least two layers of water-based paint. Lightweight paper will buckle when the paint dries, and poor-quality paper will weaken with repeated painting. Paper of any light or bright color—or white—will work well. The finished paper will be strong, because it will have absorbed wax.

Box lids, above, are covered with batiked paper.

You can use these colorful papers for making greeting cards, gift tags, holiday ornaments, plant-pot covers, party hats and masks, or to cover picture frames, books, portfolios and boxes. In fact, this method covers paper so completely, you can batik directly onto a cardboard cigar box.

When you use batiked paper for projects, you may find the finished paper is resistant to ink and water-soluble glues because of the wax it has absorbed. Use rubber cement and oil paint to make projects with batiked paper.

Equipment

- basic supplies listed on page 46

- for resist: liquid floor wax, paraffin, candle stubs or crayons (liquid floor wax does not cover as thoroughly as melted wax)

- cans for melting wax or crayons (optional)

- old paintbrushes, sponge brushes, in any width you like, or spoons or blocks (as specified in block-printing section on page 49) for applying wax

- watercolor, tempera or acrylic paints in light colors of bright yellow, bright blue, red and a dark color of navy blue, brown or black

- wide paint brushes for applying paint

- electric iron (optional)

- absorbent waste paper (optional)

Sketches of ideas for batik designs are shown on these pages. You can see the finished products on page 73.

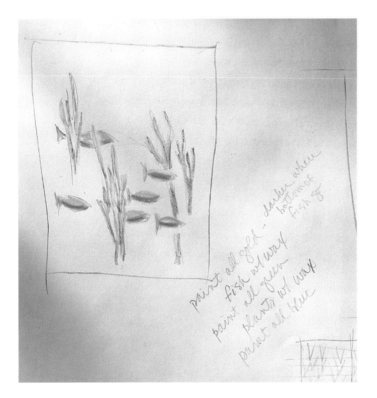

To batik

- Draw or transfer a design (following directions under Design Transfer Techniques on page 13) onto paper to be decorated.

- To use floor wax: With an old paint brush or a spoon, brush or dribble wax onto the design area that you don't want to absorb the first application of paint.

- To use melted wax: Break up paraffin, candle stubs or crayons (with paper removed) into a can; put the can in a pan of hot water over low heat on a stove or hot plate and stir until the wax is melted. Then with an old paintbrush, sponge brush or spoon, quickly apply the hot wax to the design area on the paper that you don't want to absorb the first application of paint.

- Brush the entire sheet of paper with a light color of paint. The areas covered with wax will resist the paint. Let the paint dry.

- Repeat the waxing process on areas that you want to retain the light color you've applied.

- Brush the sheet with another light color. This time, all the waxed areas will resist the paint, but the unwaxed areas will have absorbed both colors. If you've applied first yellow, then red, for example, the unwaxed background will be reddish orange. With experience, you will be able to use this process to help you achieve special effects. Let the paint dry.

- Continue to apply wax and paint until your design goal is achieved.

- If you like, paint the entire sheet with a dark shade of blue, brown or black, which can give your paper batik the appearance and "spirit" of batik fabric.

- If you've used melted wax or crayons, your paper will have a build-up of hard wax. To finish the paper, put several layers of absorbent waste paper on an ironing board, put the batiked paper over it, then cover the batiked paper with more layers of absorbent paper. With an up-and-down motion, apply a medium-hot iron to the paper so the absorbent paper will take up the excess wax. Continue changing absorbent paper and ironing until the wax is thinly distributed on the batiked paper.

The design above was made by cutting strips of lightweight cardboard into snaky shapes, placing them on beige paper, then painting the entire sheet of paper and the cardboard strips with melted wax. The strips were removed, then the paper was painted with brown paint. The waxed areas resisted the paint. This paper was used to cover a simple book shown on page 90.

The cover for the album above was decorated by coloring white paper with magenta and turquoise crayons. The colored paper was then covered with newspaper and ironed. The newspaper ink left a patina of mottled black over the design. To prevent the transfer of ink to a design, iron the newspaper first to set the ink.

Books

4 ....

Book artist Kristine Dikeman made the books on these pages. Above, a fanciful moon was stenciled onto the cover of a journal. See inside pages of this book on page 91.

Shiny orange and yellow ribbons decorate and bind a book of leaf-filled handmade paper, right. Below is a detail of the ribbon binding.

Use handmade or existing paper to make books, portfolios and albums in any size, shape or color you like. You'll find many uses for books that you make: books for guests to autograph and journals to record special events, such as milestones in a baby's life, a teenager's athletic progress, or the details of planning a wedding.

Make scrapbooks to organize news clippings or recipes, to keep photos from a family vacation, a holiday or celebration, or a family or class reunion. Make portfolios and folders to protect photos, drawings and important papers.

Equipment for all projects–

• craft knife

• scissors

• metal straightedge

• plastic, bone or wood paper folder (designed to score and rub creases in paper, these are available from well-stocked art stores)

• book board or cover material (plain or decorated oak tag, cardboard, bristol board or mat board)

For folders

- a purchased folder to use as a pattern (optional)

For books, albums and portfolios

- decorated paper or gift wrap for covers and end papers

- paper for pages—handmade, writing, construction, computer, drawing or any paper suitable for your purposes

- white glue

- paste (see recipe on page 16)

- squares of stiff cardboard to spread paste

- small brush or cotton swabs to spread paste

- weights, such as heavy books

- plastic wrap

- newspapers to protect surfaces

- awl, drill or hole punch (optional)

- vice, bulldog clips or clothespins (optional)

- binding material—strong thread, dental floss, raffia, string, thin leather strips, cotton twill tape or ribbon (optional)

- darning needle (optional)

- sewing machine (optional)

A child can make an album to keep photos of a special family outing, as at right. The cover was decorated, then pages and covers were bound by punching two holes in the top through all layers, then a leather strip was tied through the holes and their ends were weighted with baubles.

OPEN PORTFOLIO

To make a folder

Personalized or decorated folders for papers are attractive desk accessories and can give business presentations a special flair.

- Decorate cover material, like oak tag or bristol board, using any of the decorating methods described in chapter 3, "Decorating Paper."

- If you have a purchased folder that you like, you can use it as a pattern for cutting your own. Or, if you're making a folder to hold papers or photographs of unusual size, make a pattern as described below.

- To use a purchased folder as a template: Hold the folder on the undecorated side of the book board or cover material—making sure the grains of the board and the template match—and lightly trace around the folder with a pencil. Using a craft knife and metal straightedge, cut out the folder on the lines.

- To make a folder pattern: Measure the paper you will place in the folder, double the measurements, and add at least $\frac{1}{2}$ inch (12 mm) to every side.

- If you want to include a tab for identifying the folder's contents at the top or side of the folder (as is the case with most purchased file folders), add at least $\frac{1}{2}$ inch (12 mm) to the side or top measurement. If you want an envelope-style folder with closed sides, add two $\frac{1}{2}$ inch (12 mm) flaps—one to each edge of one side of the folder—which you can fold in and glue to the other side of the folder to form an envelope.

- On a large piece of scrap paper or newspaper, draw the exact shape of the folder.

- Hold the pattern on the undecorated side of the board or cover material and lightly trace around the folder with a pencil. On a work table, using a craft knife and metal straightedge, cut out the folder on the lines.

- Determine where you want the folder to fold. (If you added an extra measure for a tab, allow for the tab when you crease the folder.)

- Mark the fold line lightly with a pencil. Hold the metal straightedge along the marked line and rub the paper folder along the line, then fold along the crease.

- Protect the fold with a sheet of clean scrap paper, then rub the fold with the paper folder to sharpen the fold.

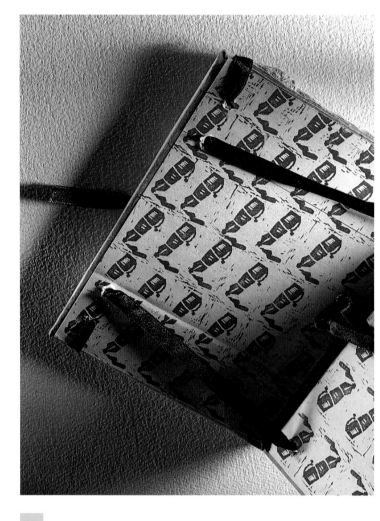

A portfolio made by Kristine Dikeman is lined with paper that was decorated with a rubber stamp and the portfolio was covered with textured handmade paper. The two covers are held together with black ribbon.

To make a portfolio

A portfolio will protect valuable papers, drawings and photographs from soil and bent corners. You can design and decorate a portfolio to reflect your desk accessories, the items it will hold, or your own inimitable personality.

You can decorate the cover material or book board directly—use mat board, bristol board or illustration board—or decorate paper to cover the boards, using any technique

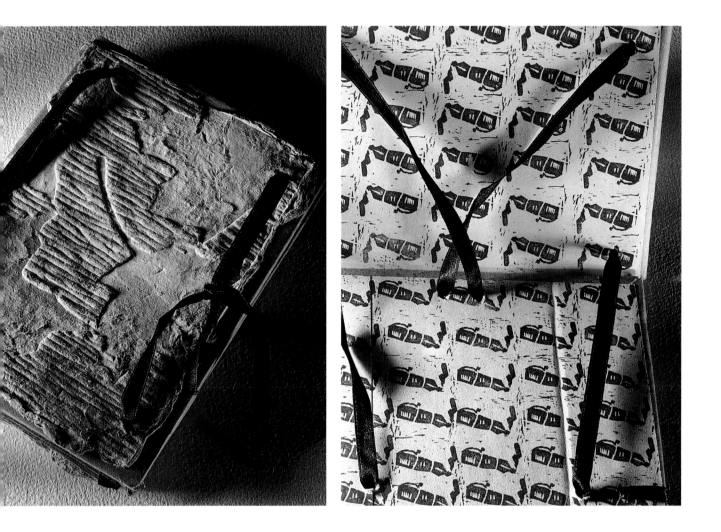

described in chapter 3, "Decorating Paper." Choose strong ribbon or cotton twill tape for tying the portfolio together.

• Determine the size of your portfolio, according to the size of the papers that it will hold. The portfolio should be cut bigger than the biggest papers that it will hold to allow some ease for them.

• Mark the size of the portfolio with light pencil marks on the book boards; place a metal straightedge on the lines and cut out with a craft knife.

• To cover boards with decorated paper: Trace around the boards you have cut out with a pencil on the undecorated side of the paper–matching the grains of board and paper. With a pencil, make lines 1 inch (2.5 cm) from each traced line. Cut the paper along the outermost lines using a straightedge and craft knife.

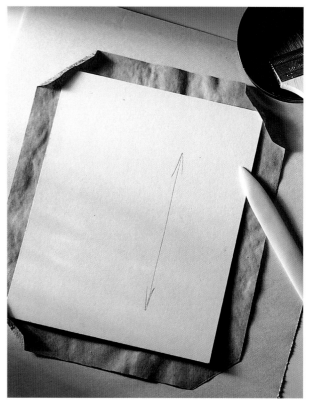

Cut a board the size you like for your portfolio or book cover, then place it on the undecorated side of the board with the grains of the board and the paper matching. (A good way to remember which way the grain lies is to draw an arrow along the lengthwise grain.) Lightly trace around the board with a pencil, making a solid line. Measure and draw dotted lines 1 inch (2.5 cm) beyond the traced lines. Measure and draw a diagonal line at each corner that equals one and-a-half times the thickness of the board. Cut the paper along the dotted cut lines, trimming off the corner triangles.

With a metal straightedge as a guide, use a bone or wooden paper folder to make creases along the solid fold lines on the cover paper, which will make folding the paper easier and more accurate. Brush one side of the board with 50/50 glue/paste mixture, then carefully lay it on the back of the paper; rub and smooth the paper. Turn the board over with the decorated side of the paper down. Apply glue to the edges of the paper. Turn one edge of the paper over the edge of the board; rub the paper down. Fold the opposite edge of the paper over the board, then fold and smooth the top, then the bottom edges of the paper.

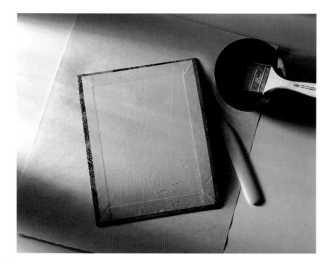

To line the cover, cut a piece of paper $\frac{1}{4}$ inch (5 mm) smaller on each side than the size of the board. Brush glue/paste over lining paper, then smooth it onto the back of the cover. Dry the cover under weights to prevent curling.

- Cover your work area with several layers of newspaper.

- Make a mixture of one part paste (see the recipe on page 16) and one part white glue.

- Apply glue/paste mixture to the book board, beginning in the center and spreading the glue out toward the edges of the board. Inevitably, you will get glue on the top sheet of newspaper, so discard that sheet and continue your work on a clean sheet of newspaper.

- Turn the glued side of the board down onto the back of the decorated paper, carefully matching the edges of the board to the traced pencil lines on the paper.

- Turn the piece over so the decorated paper is up and smooth out any wrinkles or bubbles in the paper. (To prevent smudging the paper, place a clean piece of scrap paper on top, then use your fingers and the sides of your hands to smooth the paper down.)

- Turn the board over so the decorated side is down. Trimming the corners off the decorated paper will reduce bulk when you turn the corners in. First determine the thickness of the book board. You will leave one-and-a-half times the thickness of the board at each corner of the paper. For example, if the board is $\frac{1}{4}$ inch (6 mm) thick, you will leave $\frac{3}{8}$ inch (9mm) of paper between the corner of the board and the cut line on the paper. Mark the paper $\frac{3}{8}$ inch (9mm) from each corner of the board, then mark a triangle shape. Trim off the corners at the marks.

- With a small brush or cotton swab, apply glue/paste to all the edges of the paper that will be folded over. Blot the glue with a piece of scrap paper.

- First, turn one edge of the paper over the edge of the board. Carefully but quickly smooth the paper down, and with the point of a bone or acrylic folder, rub down the paper that is folded along the edge of the board to make sure it is smooth. Fold and press down the edge of the paper on the opposite edge of the board. Now repeat the process with the top, then the bottom edges.

- To line the paper-covered boards: With a pencil, mark decorated or plain paper with measurements $\frac{1}{4}$ - $\frac{1}{2}$ inch (6-12 mm) smaller on each side than the dimensions of the boards. Be sure the grains of the paper and the book board match.

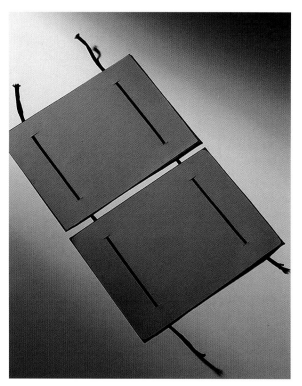

At left are two portfolios, both made with thin boards covered with decorated paper. The larger portfolio is shown open, above. To make tie closures, cut two lengths of twill tape or ribbon, each four times the width of the portfolio. Thread one tape or ribbon down through a slit in the front of the portfolio, along the underside and then up through the next slit. Repeat the process with the other tape or ribbon, then tie the portfolio closed and snip off the ends if necessary.

- Cut the paper along the lines with a metal straightedge and a craft knife.

- Using the same method for gluing as you used for covering the boards, apply glue/paste to the back of the paper, spreading the glue/paste right to the edges of the paper.

- Turn the boards with the uncovered side up and carefully position the glued side

of the liner on the back of the boards, leaving a ½ inch (12 mm) margin between each edge of the board and the liner.

- To prevent the boards from warping as they dry, dry them under weights, such as heavy books. Sandwich the boards between sheets of plastic wrap before placing the books on top. It may take two or three days for the boards to dry, depending on humidity.

- To thread ties through the portfolio: Whether or not you covered the boards with paper, determine and lightly mark with pencil the places (four on each board) where the ties will thread through the boards. The marks should be as long as the ribbon or cotton twill is wide.

- To cut the slits for the ribbon or cotton twill to run through: For each slit, carefully cut through the board with a craft knife, along the marked line; make another cut $\frac{1}{8}$ inch (3 mm) away from the first cut; then very carefully make cuts at the ends of the cut lines so you can remove the tiny pieces of board for the slits. Repeat until all eight slits are cut.

- Measure and cut the ribbon or cotton twill tape by adding: twice the width of one of the boards, plus the thickness of the portfolio when it will be filled with papers, plus 16-20 inches (40-50 cm) for tying. Cut the ribbon or twill on the diagonal or prevent fraying with a dab of glue on the cut ends.

- Lay the boards, decorated side down, side by side on a table. Thread the ribbon or twill through the slits following the illustration opposite.

- Fill the portfolio with papers or photos, then tighten the threads and tie securely.

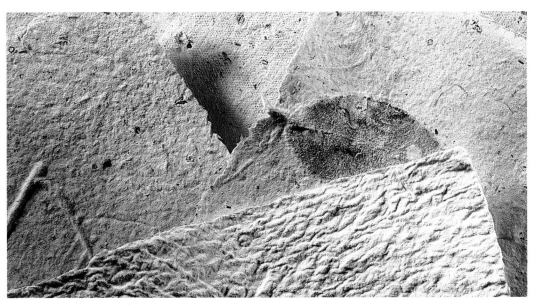

Store handmade papers in a portfolio covered with highly textured paper.

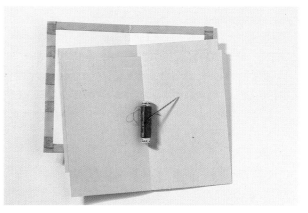

Fold sheets of paper for pages in the book. With strong thread and a needle, sew along the fold through all thicknesses, beginning and ending inside the book. Tie the thread with a square knot and trim the ends.

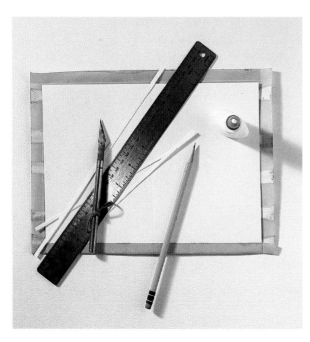

To make a single-signature book with a hand sewn binding, begin by cutting a piece of lightweight cardboard for a cover. Cut decorated paper 1 inch larger than the cardboard on all sides, fold the edges over and glue in place. Fold the cover in the center.

This process for making a book is very quick and easy. The completed book can be used as a vacation or gardening journal or for taking notes in a class.

To make a single-signature book

A single-signature book is made by folding sheets of paper in half, then sewing along the fold to hold the pages together. You can make a simple book with almost any kind of paper—typing, computer, handmade, kraft or drawing paper—and use it for writing your impressions when you travel, recording favorite recipes, or taking notes during a class.

A cover for this type of book is optional. If you don't make a separate cover, you might want to write or draw on the front and/or back to identify it. If you decide to make a

The moon shines through a page of a double-hinge book of handmade paper made by Kris Dikeman, above.

cover, the cover of the book can be made from a relatively light weight cardboard, such as oak tag, or heavy or medium weight paper, which will fold easily. The cover of your single-signature book can be the same size as the pages or slightly bigger at top, bottom and right side.

• Determine the size of your book. Remember that you will need paper for the cover and pages that is large enough to meet your dimension requirements when it is folded in half.

• You can decorate the cover material or book board in any of the methods described in "Decorating Paper," or you can cover the board with decorated paper.

The spine of this simple single-signature book was sewn on a sewing machine with the same multi-color thread that was used to create the title.

- For the cover and each page of the book, rub along the center of the page with a bone or wooden paper folder using a metal straightedge as a guide; and fold each piece of paper.

- Unfold the pages and the cover, carefully stack them with the cover on the bottom. Secure the stack with a clothespin, bull-dog clip or a vise.

- With a pencil, lightly mark where three small binding holes will be punched in the spine of the book. Make holes with an awl, drill or hole punch.

- See the illustration on page for the way to sew the binding with a needle and heavy thread, string, dental floss, raffia or narrow ribbon.

- Or, sew along the center fold on a sewing machine fitted with a heavy needle.

- Fold the book closed. The innermost pages may stick out further than the outer pages when folded. You can even up the pages by trimming off the edges with a craft knife if you like.

- To cover the book with decorated paper: On the wrong side of the decorated paper, lightly mark with a pencil the dimensions of the open book. (These lines will be used for folding lines.) Add $\frac{1}{2}$ inch (12 mm) to each side and make a cutting line. Cut along the cutting lines. Measure and mark the center of the paper where it will be folded.

You can sew a single-signature book's spine with a darning needle and strong thread, string, narrow ribbon, raffia or dental floss. To securely sew the spine, follow the arrows in this illustration.

- Hold a metal straightedge on the fold lines and the center fold line and rub along the lines with the bone or wood folder; fold all the edges toward the center.

- Unfold the decorated cover paper and place the open book on the wrong side of the decorated paper. Apply glue very lightly to the edges of the decorated paper. Blot the glue with a piece of scrap paper. (See "Adhesives for Paper" on page 14.) Fold the edges of the paper over the edges of the outside page of the book and rub the glued edges down.

To make a single-hinge book

A single-hinge on a hard bound book will let the front cover open easily. The back cover is not hinged. This is good for guest books, date books, journals, and sketch books.

For the front cover and hinge and the back cover, use a stiff board, like mat board, illustration board or bristol board.

Decorate paper for the covers in a style appropriate for your planned use for the book–formal or casual, colorful or subdued. Use any technique from chapter 3 "Decorating Paper." You'll also need plain, printed or decorated paper for lining the covers. Decorate the paper yourself or use printed gift wrap or a page from a magazine.

- Measure and mark the dimensions of the front cover on the boards you've chosen for the covers and hinge. (The cover should be ¼ inch (6 mm) larger than the pages on each side.) Now, mark a line for the hinge on the front cover. Allow the hinge panel to be wide enough to accommodate binding–at least ½ inch (12 mm) wide.

- Using a metal straightedge and craft knife, cut out the cover material or book board on the marked lines, and cut off the hinge panel for the front cover. Lay out the sheet of decorated paper or gift wrap that will cover the book.

The front of a single-hinge book opens easily, while the back cover is rigid.

- Matching the grains of the board and the decorated paper, place the cut out cover and hinge panel on the wrong side of the paper with the hinge far enough away from the cover to equal double the thickness of the board. (If the cover material is $\frac{1}{8}$ inch or 3 mm thick, allow $\frac{1}{4}$ inch or 6 mm between the cover and the hinge.) This will allow the hinge to swing open freely.

- With a pencil, lightly mark around the edges of the hinge and cover material or book board. Now treating the cover and hinge as one piece, measure those dimensions carefully. Transfer the measurements to another piece of board for the back cover of the book, but don't cut a hinge this time. The back cover's dimensions will equal the total dimensions of the hinge plus the board on the front cover.

- With a craft knife and metal straightedge, cut out the book's back cover. Again, matching the grain directions of the decorated paper and board, place the

board on the wrong side of the decorated paper and lightly make a pencil mark around the edges.

- Remove the cover material from the decorated paper for both covers. To the dimensions drawn on the decorated paper add 1 inch (2.5 cm) to allow for folding the paper over the edges of the cover.

- To cover the book's front, follow the directions for covering boards for a portfolio beginning on page 84, except treat the hinge and the cover as one piece. Then repeat these directions to cover the book's back.

Kris Dikeman's book of leaves is tied and bound with ribbon.

To bind a book

When the covers are thoroughly dry, bind the book with Japanese binding or tie binding.

- Japanese binding is effective, attractive, and easy to do. First, make a stack of paper for the pages in your book and sandwich the stack between the covers. Protect the book's covers with clean scrap paper, then secure the stack with bulldog clips or a vise.

- Measure and mark the hinge of the book to determine where the holes will be. For Japanese binding, make an odd number of holes. With an awl, drill or hole punch, make holes through the pages and both covers.

- See the illustration on page 98 for the method of threading and tying Japanese binding.

- For tie binding, make only two holes in the hinge of the book. Run a darning needle–threaded with string, heavy thread, thick or thin ribbon, leather strips or raffia–down through the top hole, under the back of the book and up through the bottom hole.

- Tie the binding material in a knot or bow on the front of the book.

To make albums and scrapbooks

If you are going to use your book for photos, art work or clippings, you need to allow extra space between the pages to accommodate the thickness of the items you put in the book. Follow the directions for making a single-hinge, Japanese-bound or tie-bound book, except add "spacers" between each page.

- To make spacers, simply cut out strips of cover material the same size as the hinge and fit them between each page in the

The covers of the book above were covered with red bookcloth and the binding was hand sewn with black leather hinges.

book. When you make holes in the hinge, you will make the holes through the covers, pages and the spacers, then run the binding material through all the layers, too.

To make a single-hinge book using bookcloth

Bookcloth will greatly strengthen the hinge of any book, journal or album that will be opened many times. Bookcloth is paper-backed fabric and can be purchased from well-stocked art supply stores

- Decide how much of the cover of the book you want to be covered with bookcloth—this can be very narrow (covering just beyond the hinge), very wide (covering half or more of the book's cover) or might even cover the entire book.

- Measure and cut out book board or cover material and a hinge as directed under "To make a single-hinge book" on page 91.

- Lightly mark on the cover material or board with a pencil where the bookcloth and the decorated paper will meet. Measure the dimensions of the board to the line you have marked plus the width of the hinge and the space between the hinge and cover.

- Also, measure and mark the dimensions of the decorated paper—at the edge where the cover meets the bookcloth, the paper will cover the edge of the bookcloth by $\frac{1}{8}$ inch (3 mm).

- For both the bookcloth and paper, add 1 inch (2.5 cm) to the top, bottom and one side of the dimensions you have measured. Matching the grain of the bookcloth, decorated paper and the book board or cover material, mark the dimensions onto the back of the bookcloth and decorated paper. With a craft knife, cut the bookcloth and the decorated paper along the marked lines with scissors.

- Make a mixture of one part white glue and one part paste (recipe on page 16), so you will have an adhesive that will dry slowly enough to give you time to work with the paper, yet thin enough to spread thinly and evenly. Apply glue/paste to the hinge and the area of the book board or cover material that will be covered with bookcloth. (See "Adhesives for paper" on page 14 for gluing tips.)

- Turn the glued side of the board and hinge down onto the back of the bookcloth, carefully matching the edges of the board to the pencil lines on the bookcloth.

- Turn the piece over so the bookcloth is up and smooth out any wrinkles or bubbles.

- Now, glue the paper onto the board. Apply glue/paste to the area of the board that will be covered with decorated paper. Also, quickly apply glue/paste to the edge of the decorated paper that will overlap the bookcloth and blot the glue/paste with scrap paper to prevent leaks.

- Turn the board or cover material and hinge down onto the back of the decorated paper, carefully matching the edges of the board to the pencil lines on the paper and making sure the paper overlaps the bookcloth by only $\frac{1}{8}$ inch (3 mm).

- Turn the piece over so the paper and bookcloth are up and smooth out any wrinkles or bubbles. (To prevent smudging the paper, place a clean piece of scrap paper on top, then use your fingers and the sides of your hands to smooth the paper down.)

- Turn the cover over so the decorated side is down. Determine the thickness of the book board or cover material. You will

trim triangle-shapes off the corners of the paper and bookcloth (to reduce bulk), leaving one and-a-half times the thickness of the board at each corner. So, if the cover material or book board is $\frac{1}{4}$ inch (6 mm) thick, you will leave $\frac{3}{8}$ inch (9 mm) of the bookcloth or paper at each corner. This will ensure that the corners are well covered.

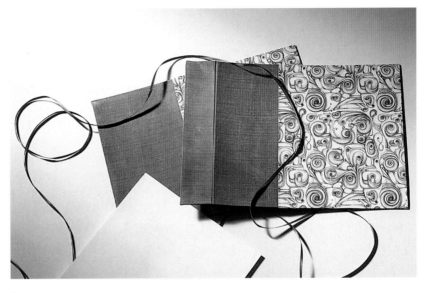

Sage green silk bookcloth covers more than a third of the covers of a single-hinge book that is ready to be filled with paper and bound with ribbon.

- With a small brush or cotton swab, apply glue/paste to all the edges of the paper that will be folded over. Blot the glue with scrap paper.

- First, turn one edge of the paper over the edge of the board. Carefully but quickly smooth the paper down, and with the point of a bone or acrylic folder, rub down the paper that is folded along the paper that is folded along the edge of the board to make sure it is smooth. Fold and press down the edge of the paper on the opposite edge of the board. Now repeat the process with the top, then the bottom edges.

- Repeat this process to make the back of the book, ignoring the references to the hinge. Be sure the bookcloth on the back of the book measures the same as that on the front of the book, so the book looks balanced.

- To dry the covers so they don't warp, make a stack consisting of

  plastic wrap
  a cover
  plastic wrap
  the other cover
  and another sheet of plastic wrap.

- Now weight the stack with heavy books. Leave until dry, which can take two or three days, depending on humidity.

To make a double-hinge book

Double-hinge books have hinges on both covers, making their spines very easy to open. To make a double-hinge book, follow the instructions under "To make a single-hinge book" on page 91, except make a hinge for both the back and front covers.

To make Japanese binding, above and below, use any strong thread or string and large-eyed needle. Begin binding by pushing the threaded needle up through a hole leaving a 3 inch (7 cm) tail of thread, then bring the thread around the side of the book, then push the needle through the same hole again. Enter the next hole by pushing the needle down, around the edge, then down through the same hole. Go to the next hole and repeat this process until you reach the last hole. Now take the thread around the lower end of the book, then work your way back to the top of the book and finally to the same hole where you began. Your Japanese binding will look like the photo above. To tie off the thread, make a tight square knot with the two ends of thread, then clip the ends. You can leave the knot at the book's back or work it into the hole.

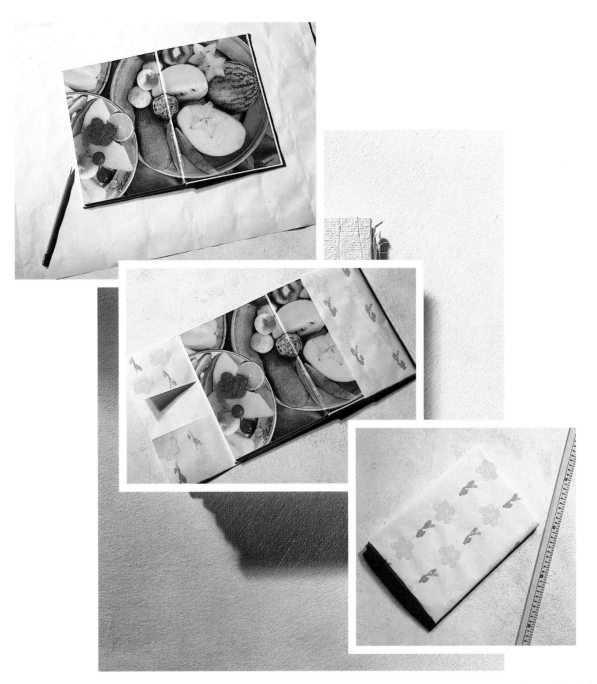

Protect a valued book by covering it with paper you have decorated. First, lay the book on the plain side of the paper and mark its top and bottom measurements with a pencil. Trim the paper, if needed, leaving a margin of paper at least 3 inches (7.5 cm) wide on every side. Fold the paper to the inside at top and bottom, then with the book's covers still open, fold in the ends, which will form pockets. Insert the book's covers into the pockets and close the book, making adjustments for fit as necessary.

Cards

5

Whether simple or ornate, a handmade card is a warm way of sending greetings for any occasion. In the time it takes to go to a card shop and choose an appropriate card, you can design and make a unique card that will be treasured by its recipient as a gift from your heart.

You can make cards and complementary envelopes with virtually any kind and size of paper and decorate them however you like.

Greeting cards can be folded once at the center or off-center, accordion folded or made in the form of booklets–sewn at the spine with thread or ribbon–or Japanese-bound. (See "To bind a book" on page 95 for details.)

Although some paper may be too porous, fine or bumpy for writing or drawing, you can use it for making cards. Decorate it by gluing bits of other papers on it; dribble melted crayons on it; block print it with paint or an ink pad; or, spray it with paint. (See chapter 3, "Decorating Paper" for details.) Then, to write a greeting on the inside, simply cut out paper that is smooth and heavy enough to be written on and glue it lightly to the inside of the card.

The greeting cards at left and on page 102 were decorated with block prints cut from rubber erasers. They could be used to send birthday or get-well wishes, or a hello note.

For envelopes that will go through the mail, use paper that can be written on easily, is smooth, strong and large enough to make an envelope that will meet post office regulations for size. If the envelope will hold a card that will be hand-delivered or enclosed in a gift box, you can make it of any paper that is large enough to accommodate the card it's designed to hold.

Create "nature" cards, above, by making handmade paper with recycled computer paper, dried ferns and flowers, then trim and fold them to fit into purchased envelopes.

Recycle cereal and other food boxes, by cutting the large box panels into postcard sizes. Write a message and apply a stamp on the back of the card.

Equipment

- paper: handmade, kraft, foil, computer, typing, drawing, watercolor, gift wrap, shopping bags or construction paper—printed, decorated or plain

- metal straightedge

- bone or wooden paper folder

- craft knife

- scissors (optional)

- white glue and/or glue stick (optional)

- wax or crayon to seal envelopes (optional)

- materials for decorating the cards: glitter, foil, tissue paper, colored paper, crayons, paint, colored pencils, paint or stencils (see chapter 3, "Decorating Paper," for more ideas)

- To make envelopes: You can make cards that are folded, sealed and addressed without an envelope, or make envelopes to match or contrast your handmade cards.

- You may have a purchased envelope that you especially like. To use it as a template, carefully pull it apart at every glued seam so that it lies flat. (If the glue is stubborn, you can hold the envelope over steam until the glue softens and pull the seams apart.)

- If the envelope is the right size for your card, you can use it as a template for cutting out an envelope from any paper that you like. Simply place the unfolded envelope on a sheet of paper, trace around its edges and cut along the lines.

4

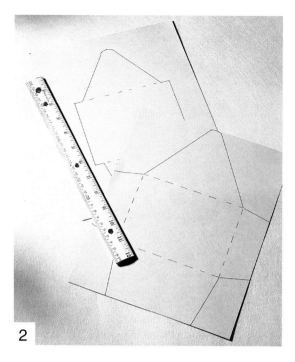

A card was made by hand sewing a foil heart onto white paper and an envelope was made from semi-transparent vellum.

1. Measure and lightly draw the dimensions of the card onto the wrong side of the envelope paper; make sure the flaps will be long enough to overlap.

2. Measure and draw the envelope flaps.

3 Cut out the envelope shape and press along the four fold lines, then, if you like, you can glue the flaps down or leave them loose.

4. Slip the card into the handmade envelope and seal with melted wax, white glue or rubber cement.

- Remove the card from the paper and with a straightedge, draw triangles using each pencil line as the base of a triangle.

The triangles must be long enough so that the points will meet and the edges will overlap to form the envelope.

- Cut along the outside lines (along the triangles) with scissors or a craft knife. Fold the template to make sure it fits the card.

- Place the template on the paper you chose for making the envelope and trace around it with a pencil. Cut along the lines with scissors or a craft knife. You might want to cut the edge of the flap with scallops or points, or cut out a shape from the flap so the card will show through.

- With a metal straightedge as a guide, rub a bone or wooden paper folder along the places where the envelope will fold. Fold the envelope and carefully apply a very small amount of white glue to the edges that will meet to make the envelope, but leave one side open for inserting the card.

- When the glued edges are dry, put the card in the envelope. You can seal the envelope with melted wax or crayons dripped onto the edge of the closed envelope, or you can glue the edge down.

The cards above were decorated with thread on a sewing machine with straight and zig-zag stitches. You could make a stack of personalized cards like these for yourself or as a special gift for a friend.

- If it is not the right size, study its shape and how it goes together so you can use its best features to make your own envelope.

- To make a template for an envelope, place a card in the center of a large sheet of paper and lightly trace around the card with a pencil. Add a $\frac{1}{8}$ inch (1 mm) margin to each side to give some ease for inserting the card into the envelope.

Quick-to-make decorations for greeting cards are shown above. From top left: a leaf shape was hand sewn onto handmade paper; foil fish and cut-outs from a paper dinner napkin were glued onto handmade paper; aluminum foil stars were glued onto white; and a foil heart was sewn onto paper by tacking it down with gold metallic thread.

• If you want to be able to lick or dampen the edge of the envelope to seal it, apply glue stick to the inner edge of the flap and let the glue dry thoroughly with the flap open. When you're ready to seal the envelope, you can lick the glue and rub the edge to seal it.

Make a handmade card even more special by mounting a photograph on its front.

1. A sheet of handmade paper was glued onto a sheet of cardstock; then they were both folded.

2. The photo was placed on the card's front and measured so that slits could be cut through the paper and the card.

3. The photo is mounted on the card by slipping the photo into the slits.

1

2

Some handmade paper is too porous or weak to write on, but would make an attractive greeting card. Line the paper with stronger paper for writing your message.
1. Find the center of the paper where it will be folded.
2. Make fold lines with a wooden or bone folder and a straightedge.
3. Put a few light dots of glue on the handmade paper, then weight the paper until the glue dries. Fold both papers together.
4. Decorate one side of the hand-made paper before you make the card, if you like. The paper, below, was block printed with black dots and white circles.

3

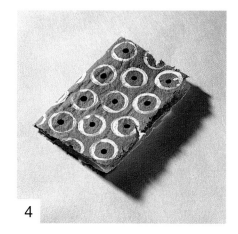

4

Laurie Middleton made the cards on this page by gluing highly textured handmade paper onto cardstock, then adding corrugated cardboard and holiday stamps from years gone by.

Boxes

6

Unattractive or scarred boxes become beautiful, useful objects when covered with paper. Round, square, lidded or open, boxes are handy in any home or office for keeping small items such as seashells, pencils, pasta, potpourri, game pieces, postage stamps, or love letters.

Any strong plain, printed, decorated, or handmade papers can be used to cover boxes. Or, make collages of paper cut from fashion magazines or colored construction paper to cover metal recipe boxes, painted or unfinished wood boxes, department store gift boxes, or cigar boxes.

Old wood is often dry and drinks glue and paste, resulting in air bubbles and an uneven finish. The solution is simple—thin white glue with water until it has the consistency of thin cream, then paint the box with the thinned glue and let it dry before covering the box.

Enameled metal boxes (like small file or recipe boxes) that are not chipped or rusted can be covered with paper, but tin cans most often contain ferrous metal, which will rust and ruin the paper covering.

If the box has a fitted lid, be sure it fits loosely enough so that when it and the box are covered, the lid won't be too tight for the box.

Use the same basic measuring, cutting and covering techniques described in this chapter to cover other objects, like trays, plates, bowls and pencil holders.

Boxes can hold jewelry, stationery, business receipts, gifts, computer disks, or art supplies. The boxes at right were decorated in various ways. Clockwise from left:

A cigar box was covered with brown paper and its top with metallic gold, then a collage was glued to the top before the whole was covered with many layers of polyurethane varnish.

A round box was covered with magazine paper, then pencils were covered with similar paper for a desk set.

Another cigar box was covered with off-white handmade paper that was made with a pressed plant added while the paper was being formed; after the paper was glued to the box, it was sprayed with protective acrylic.

Recipes and photos from a French food magazine were clipped out and glued with rubber cement to a metal recipe box, then sprayed with several coats of glossy acrylic.

Fish shapes were drawn with crayons onto white paper for the top of a small gift box, and beige tissue paper was used to cover the box's bottom.

Equipment

- box of any size and shape–with or without lid

- decorated, printed or plain paper to cover outside of box

- decorated, printed or plain paper to cover inside of box

- scrap paper

- craft knife

- scissors

- metal straightedge

- white glue

- squares of stiff cardboard to spread glue

- paste (see recipe on page 16)

- bone or wooden folder

- polyurethane varnish (optional)

- newspapers to protect surfaces

To cover a square or rectangular box

- Cut two long, thin strips of scrap paper to use for measuring the box's dimensions. Place one end of a strip of paper extending 1 inch (2.5 cm) into the bottom of the box you are covering. Pressing the strip to fold it at each angle, pull the strip up the inside, down the outside, along the bottom, up the other side and 1 inch (2.5 cm) into the bottom of the box. Make a pencil mark at every fold line on the strip.

- Repeat the measuring process above to determine the other dimension of the box.

- Lay out the strips along two adjacent edges of the paper you intend to use to cover the box.

- Transfer the pencil marks on the strips to the wrong side of the covering paper. Draw a tab extension, as illustrated above right, at the four outside corners to make sure the corners are well covered.

- Using a metal straightedge and a craft knife, carefully cut along the lines.

- Make a mixture of one part white glue and one part paste, which dries slowly and allows time for making fitting adjustments. (See recipes for paste on page 16.) Spread the glue/paste thinly on the bottom of the box.

Measure the dimensions of the box with long strips of paper. Lay out the strips of paper along adjacent edges of the covering paper and transfer the box's dimensions to the paper. Draw tab extensions on each side, which will ensure well covered corners. Cut out the cover paper.

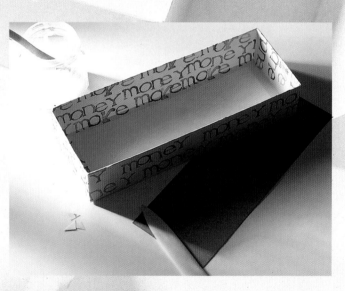

Brush a thin coat of glue/paste on the bottom of the box and place it on the wrong side of the decorated paper. Turn it over and smooth it out. Turn right side up and glue the sides of the paper that have tabs. Turn up the glued sides and rub well. Repeat with the other two sides. Cut lining paper the same dimensions as the inside of the box. Test the size, then glue the wrong side of the liner and smooth it into the bottom.

The cigar box, above, was covered with paper, then an angleic collage of magazine pictures was glued to the top before the box and lid were covered with many layers of clear varnish.

- Place the box on the center of the wrong side of the decorated paper, matching the edges of the box to the guidelines on the paper.

- Turn the box and paper over and smooth out any bubbles or tunnels, then turn the box right side up.

- Apply a thin layer of glue/paste to the sides of the paper that have tabs.

- Turn up the paper to adhere to the sides of the box, smoothing and rubbing the paper, especially at the corners where air is easily trapped. The tabs will completely cover the outside corners. To be sure the corners are securely glued, use a bone or wooden folder to push and rub the tabs in place.

- Repeat the process with the other two sides so the entire box is covered.

To line a square or rectangular box

- Place a long, thin strip of scrap paper along the inside bottom of the box, pressing the strip into the edges. Cut the strip of paper at the fold lines. Repeat for the other dimension of the bottom of the box.

- Measure the strips and, with a pencil, transfer the measurements to the lining paper. Make sure the grain of the paper is straight.

- Cut the lining paper along the lines.

- Apply a thin layer of glue/paste to the wrong side of the lining paper, spreading the glue/paste to the very edges of the paper.

- Carefully snuggle the paper into the bottom of the box and rub and smooth the lining with your fingers and press the corners with a bone or wooden folder.

Cover boxes of odd shapes, such as the purchased heart-shaped boxes, above, in the same manner as suggested for covering round boxes and lids.

To cover and line a square or rectangular lid

- Follow the same instructions for covering and lining a box (above).

- Use the same kind of paper or a matching or contrasting paper for the lid. You can also make an "inlaid" design with small squares of paper or a collage on the box and/or the lid after it's covered with paper.

To cover a round box

- Wrap a long, thin strip of scrap paper around the outside of the box and overlap it by $\frac{1}{4}$ inch (6 mm).

- Pressing to make a fold at every angle, pull another long, thin strip of paper from $\frac{1}{2}$ inch (12 mm) inside the box, along the outside and $\frac{1}{4}$ inch (6 mm) on the bottom of the box. Make pencil marks at every fold on the strip.

- Lay out the two strips of paper along adjacent edges of the paper you intend to use to cover the box. (The grain of the paper should run parallel to the top and bottom of the box.) Transfer the pencil marks from the strips to the wrong side of the paper.

- Cut the rectangle of paper along the outside pencil marks.

- Apply a thin layer of glue/paste to the outside of the box, spreading the glue/paste right to the edges of the box.

- Lay the box on the paper, carefully matching the edges of the box to the pencil guidelines—with margins of $\frac{1}{2}$ inch (12 mm) at the top and $\frac{1}{4}$ inch (6 mm) at the bottom of the box.

- Roll the box along the paper to adhere the paper to the box and smooth and rub the paper to make sure there are no air bubbles or tunnels. Apply a thin layer of glue/paste to the overlap of paper, blot it and smooth the overlap to complete the cover.

- With scissors, make snips into the top margin of the paper $\frac{1}{4}$ inch (6 mm) apart, making sure the snips don't extend beyond the edge of the box.

- Gently apply a thin layer of glue/paste to the snipped margin, and turn flaps to the inside of the box, making sure you don't tear off any of the bits of paper. Smooth them down.

- Repeat the above process to turn under the bottom margin.

To line a round box

- Use a long, thin strip of paper to measure the round dimension of the inside of the box. Overlap the strip by $\frac{1}{4}$ inch (6 mm).

- Determine the top-to-bottom dimension of the lining by pulling another long, thin strip of paper from the edge of the top, down the side and $\frac{1}{4}$ inch (6 mm) into the bottom of the box.

- Lay out the two strips of paper along adjacent edges of the lining paper. (The grain of the paper should run parallel to the top and bottom of the box.)

- Cut the rectangle of paper along the pencil marks.

- Draw a light pencil line $\frac{1}{4}$ inch (6 mm) from the bottom edge of the paper.

- With scissors, make snips in the paper $\frac{1}{4}$ inch (6 mm) apart from the bottom edge to the line drawn $\frac{1}{4}$ inch (6 mm) from the edge of the paper.

- Apply a thin layer of glue/paste to the wrong side of the paper, spreading the glue/paste right to the edges and being careful not to tear off the snipped bits of paper.

- Carefully matching the top of the lining to the top edge of the box, smooth and press the lining to the inside of the box, overlapping the lining $\frac{1}{4}$ inch (6 mm) and pressing the snipped edge smoothly on the bottom of the box. Use a bone or wooden folder to make sure the edges are all smooth.

The smaller round box at left was covered with paper batiked with blue and metallic gold; the larger box was covered with a city road map.

- Measure the bottom diameter of the box by laying a long, thin strip of paper along the bottom of the box. Press the paper into the edges to make folds in the paper. Cut the paper at the folds.

- Make a template by drawing a circle with the same diameter as the length of the strip of paper onto a piece of scrap paper.

- Carefully trace around the template on the wrong side of the paper you have chosen as lining for the inside of the box. While you're at it, use the same template to make a circle of paper to cover the outside bottom of the box.

- Apply a thin layer of glue/paste to the wrong side of the circle of paper for the inside bottom and carefully snuggle it into the box. Press and smooth the lining with your fingers and with the bone or wooden folder to make sure all the edges are securely glued.

- Apply a thin layer of glue/paste to the wrong side of the circle of paper for the outside bottom. Turn the box bottom-side up and carefully fit the circle of paper onto the bottom of the box. Let it dry.

To cover a round lid

- Follow the same instructions for covering and lining a round box (above).

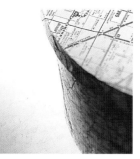

- Use the same kind of paper or a matching or contrasting paper for the lid. You can also make an "inlaid" design with small squares of paper or a collage on the top of the lid after it's covered with paper.

Finishing boxes and lids

Many papers adhered to boxes are best left as they are, especially if the papers are very strong or have interesting textures. But, in the case of collages or thin papers, you may want to apply a protective polyurethane finish. An advantage to a polyurethane finish is that it will make the box water-resistant.

- Polyurethane will permanently darken paper when it's applied directly. To prevent this, mix white glue with water until it has the consistency of thin cream, then brush the paper-covered box with a thin coat of the glue. Let it dry completely.

- With a soft brush, gently apply a thin layer of the polyurethane to the box, making sure there are no air bubbles or lumps; let it dry overnight.

- To give a collage a perfectly smooth surface, apply many coats of polyurethane. Lightly rub the box with fine sandpaper after each coat is thoroughly dry, and wipe off the dust with a damp cloth before brushing on another coat. Continue until you can run your hand along the dry surface and feel no bumps.

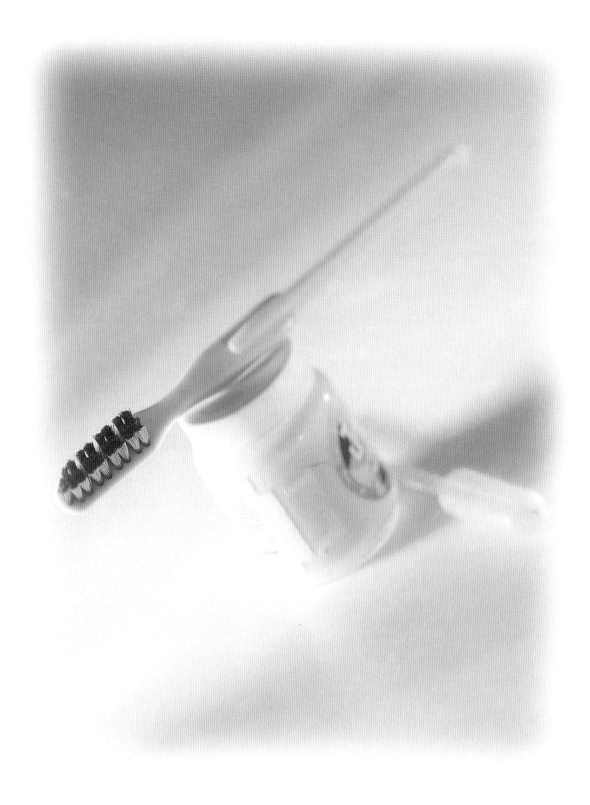

Frames

Give new life to old frames by covering them with paper. You can also revitalize picture mats that are worn or stained, or cover plain purchased mats with decorated or printed paper to enhance a framed object. In a specially designed frame with a complementary mat, a beloved photograph, drawing, painting or even a postcard can become a work of art.

The next time you visit a gallery or art museum, pay attention to the ways frames and mats are used to enhance artwork. You'll find that there are no strict rules about frame size, color or material and that mats are made of many materials in many sizes. In most cases, however, the frame treatment is in keeping with the "tone" of the art–formal, funky, traditional, pastoral or primitive.

The first step in designing a frame and mat is to choose the item to be framed. Consider the size, shape, colors and textures that will enhance the object. Take out samples of paper you made from chapter 2,

Make special frames for your favorite pictures, drawings and memorabilia. An inexpensive acrylic frame, above, was lined with a sheet of handmade paper that was cut to frame a treasured family photo.

Opposite, a scarred wooden frame was covered with white tissue paper that was first dipped in dilute white glue, then applied to the frame and moved and bunched to give a soft, marbled effect. See page 132 for directions.

"Handmade Paper," or papers you decorated in any of the ways suggested in chapter 3, "Decorating Paper," or printed or decorated papers, like gift wrap, magazine pages or marbled papers you have purchased. Spread these samples out on a table in good light and decide which of these look best with the item you will frame.

Now, look at various colors and textures to use as a mat or to cover an existing mat. Look at the way various mat widths affect the item to be framed–in most cases, a wide mat looks best with a large item. But experiment. Sometimes a huge mat surrounding a small photo can make the photo look more important.

Equipment

- picture frame to cover, or heavy cardboard or foamcore to cut and cover

- glass, plexiglass or acetate cut to fit the frame (optional)

- light- or medium-weight paper–plain, printed or decorated–to cover the frame

- pre-cut mat (optional)

- light- or medium-weight paper–plain, printed or decorated–to make a mat or to cover an existing mat

- medium-weight card for backing

- craft knife for cutting paper

- metal straightedge

- architect's triangle with a 45° angle

- white glue

- paste (see recipes on page 16)

- plastic wrap

- weights such as heavy books

- bone or wooden paper folder

- paper tape

- eyelet screws and picture wire for wall hanging (optional)

Three sheets of handmade paper were professionally mounted on golden brown mat board and framed with maple.

Frames

Old wood frames may be very dry and porous. Before covering these frames with paper, coat them with a layer of thinned white glue and let it dry thoroughly before applying paper. If you're covering a metal frame, make sure there are no rust spots, which would eventually ruin the paper covering. Rub any rust spots with sandpaper, then spray the metal with a rust preventative.

The smooth or textured paper you choose to cover frames can be light- or medium-weight, manufactured or handmade, printed, decorated or plain.

Mats

Mats add a dimension of color and/or texture to a photo or drawing. Depending on your style and the style of the item you're framing, the mat can be colorful, refrained, primitive, abstract, or traditional. As a general rule, make a mat with a color that is in the picture, but is not dominant. You can layer mats to introduce various colors and textures. Personalize mats in any of the ways suggested for decorating paper in chapter 3, "Decorating Paper."

Cutting thick mat board accurately is nearly impossible without a mat cutter. If you don't have a mat cutter, buy a pre-cut mat the size you need for your project—or recycle an old mat—and cover it with paper that will enhance the frame and object you're framing. Consider making a mat of paper, rather than mat board. Like a mat cut from board, a carefully cut paper mat can add extra color and/or texture to a framed presentation.

To cut a frame from cardboard or foamcore

Make a simple frame any size or shape you like by cutting it from heavy cardboard or foamcore. You can make frames in the shapes of hearts, circles, animal forms, bows, flowers, bicycles, cowboy hats—whatever shape you like. And, you can cut out one or more windows to display pictures. Measure, mark, then cut the material with a craft knife. Decorate the frame in any of the ways described in this chapter.

Here's a great way to cover a beat-up wooden frame, above, or a frame cut from cardboard or foamcore. Lea Blake tore magazine pages into narrow strips, then glued them onto an old frame in a diagonal design.

A quick way to mount the picture or object in the frame is to back it with a sheet of lightweight cardboard cut to a size that is big enough to back the picture but will not extend beyond the frame's outside edges. Position the lightweight cardboard on the back of the frame, then secure one edge of the cardboard with tape. (It will swing open and closed like a book.) Place the picture between the backing and frame, then tape the backing on all four sides.

These frames are lightweight enough to hang on the refrigerator; just glue a magnet to the frame's back.

To hang the frame on the wall or to stand it on a table, see instructions under "Finishing a frame for hanging" or "Finishing a table frame."

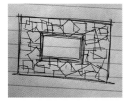

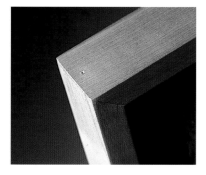

Shown above are the elements you need to decorate a frame: an idea, supplies, including interesting paper, and an existing frame. The plan illustrated above is to make a mosaic of handmade papers glued onto paper then onto a wood frame.

Covering a Frame

Strips and stripes

- Cut or tear papers of two or more colors into strips that are long enough to wrap the frame in straight lines or on the diagonal. Thin white glue with water, brush the thinned glue onto the back of a strip of paper, and apply it to the frame. Repeat with the strips of cut or torn paper until the frame is covered.

- Finish and protect the frame with spray-on or paint-on polyurethane or brush with two layers of thinned white glue, allowing it to dry thoroughly between applications.

All-over cover

- Use a narrow strip of paper to measure the width of the frame. If the frame has grooves and high points, be sure to rub the measuring strip into all the grooves. Wrap the strip so that the paper starts and finishes at least $\frac{1}{4}$ inch (6 mm) on the back of the frame for an overlap allowance. With a ruler, measure the dimensions of the outside and inside of the frame.

- Smooth the paper measuring strip out and transfer the measurement of the frame onto the back of the decorated paper with light pencil lines. Also, carefully transfer the inside and outside dimensions of the frame onto the paper.

- With a craft knife and a metal straightedge, cut out the outside dimensions and then cut out a window along the dimensions of the inside (including the overlap allowance.)

- To reduce bulk at the corners of the frame, allow a margin equal to the width of the frame, then mark lightly with a

frame on the glued side of the paper; turn the frame right-side up and smooth the paper onto the frame, making sure the paper is rubbed into all the grooves of the frame.

A battered plastic frame with a heart cut-out was covered quickly with handmade paper glued onto the old frame, right.

pencil on the wrong side of the covering paper a line to cut off triangles at each corner. Cut off the triangles with a craft knife or scissors. At each corner of the "window," cut slits just to the corner where the paper will overlap the frame.

- With a brush or the edge of a square of cardboard, lightly spread a 50/50 mixture of white glue and paste (see recipes on page 16) on the back of the cover paper. Working carefully and quickly, place the

- Turn the frame so its back is toward you and carefully turn the overlap to the back of the frame, turning corners to miter.

When the frame is dry, protect it, if you like, with one or more coats of spray or brush-on polyurethane.

Textured tissue

- Choose a color of tissue paper that matches or contrasts with the frame you are covering. Cut the tissue paper into four strips; each strip should be wide enough to wrap around the frame's width with an overlap to go around the back of the frame, and about $1\frac{1}{2}$ times longer than each of the frame's sides.

- In a shallow bowl, thin white glue with water so it has the consistency of milk. Dip one of the strips into the glue and apply it to one side of the frame. (The wet tissue paper will be fragile.) Scrunch up the tissue paper so it looks crumpled and gently rub the paper into any grooves in the frame and press the overlap to the back of the frame. Rinse the glue off your fingers periodically to prevent tearing the paper–but if tears occur, you can cover them with little bits of tissue paper. Repeat with the other strips of paper until the frame is covered. Let it dry. The finish will be hard but not shiny. If you want a glossy finish, brush or spray on high-gloss polyurethane.

Mosaic

- You can achieve many different effects by cutting or tearing paper and applying the pieces to a frame with white glue thinned with water. Use magazine pictures, newspaper, gift wrap, kraft paper, handmade paper or tissue paper. Cover the entire frame or allow parts of the frame to show.

- It's a good idea to arrange the pieces of paper on the frame before you glue them down to make sure they fit and that you like how they look.

- Dip the pieces of paper in white glue thinned to the consistency of milk, then apply them to the frame. The papers can be layered, and other objects, such as buttons, silk flowers, ribbon, rickrack, snips of thin copper or brass sheeting or wire, lace, or beads, can be glued onto the frame with the paper.

- Spray or brush the frame, after it dries, with matte or high-gloss polyurethane.

Finishing a Frame for Hanging

Hardware stores carry several styles and sizes of picture hanging options. The easiest and most effective are two eyescrews or D-rings and braided picture wire. Use screws the size that are appropriate for the size and weight of the picture. You can also purchase metal picture hangers to put in the wall, rather than hanging pictures on nails, which often damage the wall.

- For eyescrews or D-rings, start holes about one-third the way down from the top of the frame, then screw in the eyescrews. Be careful that the end of the screw doesn't go through the face of the frame.

- Cut a length of braided wire about 12 inches (30 cm) longer than the the frame is wide. Run one end of the wire through one of the eyescrews and pull about 3 or 4 inches (7 to 10 cm) through, then wrap the excess wire around the main part of the wire. Run the other end of wire through the other eyescrew, leave a bit of slack in the wire, then wrap the end of the wire around the main wire.

Finishing a Table Frame

- To make the back for a free-standing table frame, carefully measure the inside back of the frame and cut a piece of heavy cardboard to fit. Cover the cardboard with paper using a light coating of a mixture of glue and paste in the same method as used in covering portfolio covers (page 86).

- Make the stand by cutting a necktie shaped piece of cardboard. To make a hinge to allow the stand to bend, carefully cut a very shallow line in one side of the cardboard, using a metal straightedge and craft knife, about 1 inch (2.5 cm) from the top of the stand. Cover the stand with the same paper. Glue the hinge section at the top of the stand to the frame back.

- Cut a strip of ribbon, twine or heavy paper to hold the stand up. Before gluing it to the stand and back, experiment with the length of the ribbon to see how it looks. Secure the back to the frame with small brads.

From heavy cardboard, cut a neck-tie shape for the back of a table frame. Make a hinge by carefully slitting one layer of the cardboard with a craft knife. Cover the board with paper in the same manner used to cover boards for a portfolio, as described on page 86.

Attach the stand by gluing the hinge piece to the back of the frame, then cut a short length of ribbon or twill that is just long enough to hold the frame upright, and to prevent the stand and frame from separating.

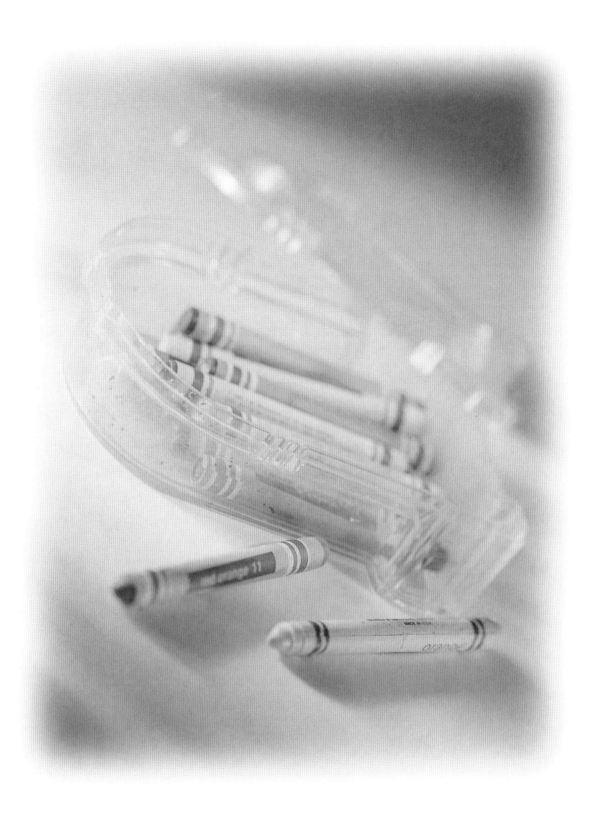

Gallery

Use greeting cards to make tiny gift boxes, as shown on these pages. Simply cut a card apart and into shapes, if you like. Then glue edges of the card together, leaving an opening at the top. Stuff a bit of tissue paper or shredded paper into the box before adding a small gift, such as candy, jewelry or perfume.

Kris Dikeman made the paper and books shown on this page. To the handmade paper bound into the book at left, she put lengths of colored threads in still-wet paper. When the paper and threads were pressed together, they became enmeshed. Kris used strands of bright, shiny ribbons to decorate and bind the book above.

Glue paper to a terra cotta flower pot, then paint inside and outside with several layers of polyurethane to waterproof the pot.

*Send a love note in a handmade envelope made
of vellum and sealed with red wax~and a kiss.*

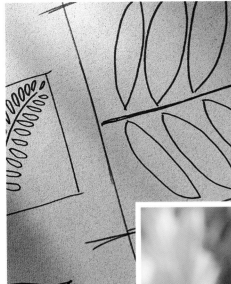

Paper flowers can brighten a corner of a room or help create a festive mood for a party. Fold and cut tissue paper, then spread the petals of the paper flowers and tie at the base with thin wire.

Press wet pulp onto the bottoms of inverted bowls or water glasses to make paper containers. Prepare the bowls or glasses by spraying well with non-stick vegetable cooking spray, which will allow the dried pulp to release without damaging the paper.

Hand bookbinding is a special skill and art that can result in beautiful, long-lasting projects, as illustrated by the book above.

Index